Somewhere Bluebirds Fly
An Adoptee's Search for Home

by Rick Farrant

DORRANCE PUBLISHING CO
EST. 1920
PITTSBURGH, PENNSYLVANIA 15238

The contents of this work, including, but not limited to, the accuracy of events, people, and places depicted; opinions expressed; permission to use previously published materials included; and any advice given or actions advocated are solely the responsibility of the author, who assumes all liability for said work and indemnifies the publisher against any claims stemming from publication of the work.

All Rights Reserved
Copyright © 2020 by Rick Farrant

No part of this book may be reproduced or transmitted, downloaded, distributed, reverse engineered, or stored in or introduced into any information storage and retrieval system, in any form or by any means, including photocopying and recording, whether electronic or mechanical, now known or hereinafter invented without permission in writing from the publisher.

Dorrance Publishing Co
585 Alpha Drive
Suite 103
Pittsburgh, PA 15238
Visit our website at *www.dorrancebookstore.com*

ISBN: 978-1-6480-4293-5
eISBN: 978-1-6480-4886-9

To Lynn, Lauren, and Amber

When Comes My Day

And when I go, for go I must
I shan't mind being "dust to dust"
You know I've loved this good brown earth
The trees and flowers it gave them birth
And fed them well and rain and sun
Their opulence made the cycle run
So true to form it is God's way
So do not mourn when comes my day
To go. Relive the happy times
We had. The friends in many climes
The jokes and then sometimes the tears
But rarely – for throughout the years
Our blessings far outnumbered woes
So think back and remember those
Then think ahead, plan for the morrow…

Betty Wilson Farrant

Preface

Every person who has searched for biological relatives has a story. Every story is unique.

As people learned about my own search, they shared their discoveries. A woman in her sixties invited me for coffee to tell me about finding her biological mother—and the somewhat tenuous relationship that developed between the two. A woman in her early forties shared with me that she learned through an adoption agency that she had been the product of a rape when her mother was seventeen; her opposition to abortion in instances of rape was predictable. A woman in her twenties who was orphaned in Russia found out through an open-source genealogy database that many of her ancestors were of Iranian descent. A woman in her thirties discovered that she had an older half-sister who was conceived by her mother during an out-of-wedlock relationship.

The proliferation of open-source databases, other online discovery tools, and televised genealogy searches have encouraged millions of people worldwide to explore their ancestries. The outcomes have led to a range of reactions, but often there is a surprise of some sort in a person's lineage.

Mine is one person's story in a sea of discoveries that is helping shape our knowledge about our origins and connections with others.

– Rick Farrant

Chapter One

June 2017

Dear Barbara May,

I just received the black-and-white pictures of you. They're flat-toned and some are a bit cloudy, but there you are nonetheless. And I can't stop looking at you, can't stop thinking that you and I may have been one once.

I want to cry and smile at the same time. I want to reach through the images and touch you. I want to hear your voice, your laughter. I want to watch you walking or playing or sleeping. I want to ask you all sorts of questions, but mostly I want to know if you are my mother.

I search every little detail in your pictures, as if that will somehow bring me closer to you, somehow give me a better understanding of who you are—or were. I compare my facial features to yours and think, yes, the thick eyebrows, the slope of the nose, the long jaw line look a lot like mine. I'm overwhelmed by the possibility that I may have finally found you.

I don't know a lot about you yet, but the pictures, sent by your niece Carol, are beginning to tell your story, and maybe mine too.

Here's a picture of you when you were seven or eight years old in 1940, sitting on a tree stump with legs crossed at the ankles, hands resting in your lap. You're wearing a white halter dress with wide straps and a bow on one side of your straight, dark hair, which is cropped just below the ears and parted on the other side. Your impish grin lurks beneath your thick eyebrows, belying your sedate, young-lady-like posture. And I wonder, did you know then what you wanted to be when you grew up? Was your world carefree and safe and filled with joy? Were you, despite the careful pose, a rambunctious tomboy?

Here's one from 1950 when you were 17 or 18, after your mother died at the age of 39. Your hair is curly and a little wild. You smile broadly, one eyebrow slightly raised, and there's still a bit of up-to-no-good in that smile, in those lively eyes. And I wonder, were you struggling then to figure out what it meant to be a young woman? Did you feel as pretty as you looked or were you self-conscious about those two big front teeth and your nearly six-foot stature? Did you have adoring crushes on boys the way teenage girls do? Did you like listening to Nat King Cole's chart-topping "Mona Lisa," she of the mystic smile hiding, perhaps, a broken heart?

Then there are these three pictures from 1951 when you were 18, maybe 19, and resembling, at least in one photo, Mona Lisa. You've tamed your shoulder-length curls into shiny, luxurious waves—like something out of a sheen-touting shampoo commercial of the era—and you are poised, mature, and wearing lipstick. One picture looks like a high school yearbook photo, another is you in your graduation cap and gown, and the third was taken on Easter Sunday, with you wearing a big-buttoned coat, straw hat with a giant bow, and small, crescent-shaped earrings. That sepia tone-like photo was taken from the side and you seem to be enveloped by a nearby evergreen. You're looking at something in the distance, head tilted upward, lips parted in a smile. You are beautiful, elegant and confident-looking. And I wonder, in that horizon-scanning moment were you dreaming beyond the train tracks, farm fields, quaint shops, and historic churches of your childhood? Did you know what love is or were you still searching for its elusive essence? Had you already had your first kiss, your first boyfriend? Did life seem full of grand possibilities and great promise?

That year was the year before the unthinkable happened—a circumstance my birth mother, perhaps you, couldn't have imagined, couldn't have dreamt. How hard that must have been in 1952 America, when many unwed mothers were shuttled off to facilities where some of them would, in shameful exile, feel their babies grow and kick and then endure the pain of childbirth with little prospect of reward other than the hope that their newborns would grow up safe and loved. When such things were often dark family secrets, held closely by a few, and then vanquished by the passage of time and mortality. When unwed pregnant mothers were branded as morally compromised—sinful, really. I wonder and have wondered for a long time, did you, if you are my birth mother, feel lonely, lost, confused and bereft of joy? Did you love my biological father and did his abandonment leave you suspicious of men? Did you lose your beautiful smile, and did the sparkle in your eyes dim? If only briefly, did you hold your baby boy, feel the beat of his heart, look into his blue eyes, and consider that you and he might be able to make it on your own? Did you think about him when, decades later, the life in you began to ebb?

If you are my birth mother, you can't answer those questions now, at least not without divine intervention. I learned that on May 27, 2005—your birthday— you laid your head on the desk where you worked and died at the age of 73. Your obituary said you were officially survived by a husband, three daughters, a son (not me), three sons-in-law, an older sister, two nieces, and eight grandchildren. You are now buried with your husband in a sprawling country veterans' cemetery in Wrightstown, N.J. beneath a bronze plaque:

PARKER M BOHN SR
CM2 US Navy
JAN 10 1918 JULY 13 2008

BARBARA M HIS WIFE
MAY 27 1932 MAY 27 2005
ALWAYS IN OUR HEARTS

And always loved, not just by those who shared your life in full, but perhaps by a little boy whom you never really knew but to whom you may have granted the chance for life—a life you wagered would be better than the life you could have provided just a year out of high school.

For most mothers, I imagine, giving up a child must be extraordinarily painful and if I could have back in 1952, I would have wiped away your tears. I would have hugged you and whispered that everything was going to be all right. I would *have filled the emptiness that must have consumed you. I would have clung to you and healed your wounds.*

I'm pretty sure of that, Barbara May, and if you'll stick with me, I'll tell you more about me. And along the way, I'm hoping you'll in turn be able to tell me, through the scattered traces of your life, that I am your son.

Rick

Chapter Two

Throughout much of my adult life, I had a recurring fantasy that anytime an older woman seemed particularly friendly to me, she might be my biological mother. These women were bank tellers, convenience store clerks, teachers, and company presidents. They had nice smiles and nurturing natures. My imagination convinced me, preposterous as it might sound, that one of them might be following me as I crisscrossed the country for a string of journalism jobs, just to make sure my life was on a positive trajectory, which was in doubt for more than a few years.

I don't know if such a comforting fantasy is common for people who have been adopted, but in my case I suppose it was rooted in an inherent desire to know that my birth mother's love for me was enduring—that I was not forgotten.

I know I was loved in the beginning because by giving me up for adoption, my birth mother chose a more stable living environment for me than she believed she could provide. I have always been grateful for this.

The fantasy of the traveling mother, meanwhile, allowed me to imagine my birth mother any way I wanted—and usually it was in a positive way, because I couldn't fathom a neglectful, uncaring mother. That would somehow diminish my value as a person, my sense of worth. Loving her in a warm abstract didn't fully satisfy my often-suppressed desires to know who she was, but it got me through.

Until my mid-thirties, I didn't know anything about her, and what I learned then was only scant, non-identifying information provided by the adoption agency. I didn't know what she looked like. I didn't know what she sounded like. I didn't know her name. I didn't know the nuances of her personality—or much of anything about her personality for that matter.

None of that information was provided in court papers filed just before my adoption in the "closed adoption" state of New York. My adoptive mother had given me the documents after I turned twenty, and my birth mother and the circumstances of my fate were described in dispassionate, run-on legalese bereft of illuminating description:

> That, upon information and belief, the said minor above named was committed to the care and custody of The Spence-Chapin Adoption Service of 304 East 33rd Street, in the Borough of Manhattan, City, County and State of New York, on or about January 3, 1953, for the reason that the mother of said child, having sole custody of the child, was unable to provide for him and wished to have him placed in a good home where he would be cared for, and for that purpose voluntarily and unconditionally surrendered said minor to the care and custody of The Spence-Chapin Adoption Service; that the father of said child, prior to said surrender, had deserted both the child and the mother; that no inquiry has been made as to the welfare of said infant and no board has been paid by his parents, and no provision has been made by the parents, guardians, or relatives of said infant for his support and maintenance, but the parents of said child have abandoned him.

Abandoned. Such a harsh and finite-sounding word. Not lovingly abandoned. Not abandoned with regret. Not abandoned after thoughtful consideration. Simply abandoned. Without provision. Thrust into an uncertain world and future. Rudderless and without anchor.

When I first read the description of my adoption, I fought to believe that my birth mother wouldn't have written it that way if she'd had the chance. Nevertheless, in the rare moments when I dwelled on the language, I felt like little more than a thing. Something barely human and of marginal value. Many years later, I would come to realize the pervasive impact that had on my life-long feelings of unworthiness. I wasn't just given up. I was abandoned.

The court papers—which went on at great length—and other related documents offered no more information about my birth mother other than she was of the Protestant faith. Religious affiliation was apparently an important consideration in adoptions back then. Unsaid, and probably taken for granted, was the matter of race. My adoptive parents were white. I presumed my birth mother and father were white too.

The legal documents, contained in a folded, light-blue paper packet and filed with the Surrogate's Court in New York County, were signed by my adoptive parents, Lawrence and Elizabeth Farrant, when I was placed in the Farrant household on May 20, 1953, and later on April 23, 1954 when I was formally adopted and given the name Richard Farrant, no middle initial. A fee of $350 was paid. By today's standards, that would be a steal for adopting a baby.

Nowhere in the documents could I find my birth mother's name or signature, although surely she must have signed something at some point. One curious thing the papers did have was a name, Richard Alan Shinn—the name of the child being adopted. It is a name that meant little to me for most of my life. Certainly not when I was born on December 4, 1952 in Yonkers, New York or thirty days later when the adoption agency became my guardian.

By then, I had observed, somewhere and with someone, my first Christmas. I had also, somewhere and with someone, ushered in a new year that would see Dwight D. Eisenhower assuming the U.S. presidency, Soviet dictator Josef Stalin dying, an armistice signed ending the Korean War, the first sale of color television sets, and Arthur Miller's *The Crucible* opening on Broadway. What that Christmas and New Year's must have been like for my birth mother I can only imagine—and grieve along with her. It must have been a time of loss and faint hope.

No writings or photos survive to document my birth mother's life then, but my early years in the Farrant home *are* chronicled in a photo album assembled by my adoptive mother. It includes a little handmade card with a photo of her holding me. Her smile is radiant, her thick dark hair is pulled back, and she is wearing a high-collared blouse and sweater. There isn't a line on her face. The photo is accompanied by these handwritten words: "I've Been Adopted! My name is Richard. I was born on Dec. 4, 1952. I'm 28 inches tall. I weigh 21 pounds. My parents are Betty & Larry Farrant. Aren't they Lucky!" The photo is undated, as are the other photos—oddly cut out in the shapes of diamonds, clubs and spades, but no hearts—that depict a chubby-faced toddler in scuffed saddle shoes playing with a toy on a New York City sidewalk, or sitting in pajamas in a leather living room chair and pointing to a baby bottle filled with milk, or wading bare-chested in water off the New Jersey shore near my grandmother's summer house in Union Beach.

I don't remember much about those toddling years, but I'm smiling a lot in the pictures and appear to be happy. My father, already balding, is in some of the pictures and he, too, is smiling. It is a smile I don't remember. What I do remember is walking amidst the horseshoe crabs and slimy strands of washed-up seaweed in Union Beach and I remember what's in the foreground of the baby bottle photo: a rather large, golden, curly-maned stuffed lion. That lion, one of my favorite belongings, remained with me—or at least in our house—for many years. Until the stuffing began oozing from its body and its glass-button eyes fell out. Until someone must have tossed the poor dilapidated creature in the trash.

My early childhood memories, perhaps like all childhood memories, are curious, amounting to a disjointed collection of moments both significant and trivial. But even my most ordinary recollections must be rooted in some import. Why else would I still think of them all these years later?

One thing that left an indelible impression was the apartment where we lived in Manhattan—a thirteenth floor "penthouse" in a brick complex called Knickerbocker Village on Monroe Street between the Manhattan and Brooklyn bridges. Even today, I remember most of the layout vividly: my bedroom, the tiny kitchen and dining nook, a bathroom, and a living room that opened to a French-doored patio with a rather high brick enclosure and a view of the East River. For the longest time, it seemed, I could not see over the enclosure without someone holding me up or without standing on my tiptoes.

One of my earliest memories was a friend I had when I was about four. He was two years older than I was and the son of a couple my adoptive parents knew. One day, walking down the hallway of our apartment, I asked my mother, "Will I ever be the same age as Ari?" My mother smiled and said, "No honey, he will always be two years older than you." It took me at least a couple more years to fully understand why Ari would always be older. Even simple math was never my strong point.

Among my other early memories was the day I threw a large metal toy car—

a birthday present—through the window of my bedroom for reasons I don't remember. The car landed on the sidewalk thirteen stories below, miraculously hitting no one. On another day, I went to the concrete park across the street to throw a tennis ball at a wall—the beginnings of my love affair with pitching—and forgot the ball. My mother, watching from the patio, understood from my dramatic gestures what had happened and with nearly perfect aim tossed a tennis ball from her lofty perch. It cleared the street below, landed on the concrete several feet from me, and bounced what seemed like a mile high. Lots of things looked a mile high when I was four-foot-something.

In hindsight, my life was alternate worlds of highs and lows—the high world where we lived, ate and slept, and the low world where adults worked and children played and went to school. Worlds connected by an old, gated, self-service elevator that periodically got stuck between floors, creating heart-palpitating adventures for those inside.

Some of my most enduring memories of adolescence in New York City are wrapped up in my adoptive parents' unspoken insistence that I learn how to be independent. And more specifically, independent as an only child. There were no brothers or sisters to watch over me. Sometimes, there weren't even parents to watch over me. Larry and Betty, both well-studied, fancied themselves as intellectuals, he a reporter and editor for the *New York World-Telegram and Sun* and she a high school English teacher. They were both exceedingly precise in their language and mannerisms, were rarely carefree, and seemed to have a cerebral, sometimes flawed strategy for raising a child. They also had a very active social life. When I was about six they started leaving me home alone when they went out at night, usually to visit acquaintances elsewhere in our apartment building to talk, drink, and play bridge. They implored me to keep the front door locked and let no one in, reminded me to turn on nothing in the kitchen or venture to the patio, and suggested I tuck myself in when I grew sleepy. They also left phone numbers where they could be reached.

Most nights when my parents left, I would pull a chair up to the front of an old stand-up radio in the living room, turn the dial to rock 'n roll stations, and dance while holding tightly to the radio's wood frame. A young Murray the K was my favorite disc jockey. "Charlie Brown" by the Coasters and "16 Candles" by the Crests were among my favorite songs. On those nights in front of the radio, the disc jockeys, the musicians, and the singers became my guardians and my friends. In my mind, they were speaking and singing only to me.

Most nights alone passed uneventfully and I was fast asleep in my bed by the time my parents got home. But one night, I awoke feeling queasy, leaned over the side of the bed and deposited the spaghetti dinner I had eaten earlier. It landed on the wood parquet floor virtually intact, nearly undigested. Trembling, I walked to the phone, dialed the number my parents had given me, and blurted to the woman who answered, "I just threw up." The woman, a loud, heavily lipsticked socialite named Florence, said, "Who is this?" "Ricky," I answered. It was a name my mother and father preferred, at least in my adolescence, and a name I thoroughly detested.

My parents rushed back to the apartment to tend to me that night, but for the rest of my life I feared—and avoided if at all possible—throwing up. The violent upheaval of that moment never left me.

By the age of seven, my involuntary march to independence moved to the city's streets. When my parents' work schedules interfered with driving me to my private school in Brooklyn, I rode the subway by myself with lunch box in hand. Again, I was armed with instructions: don't talk to anyone, don't stand at the edge of the platform, and go directly to school. I obeyed, but my memories of those underground journeys are strobe-like and grim: homeless men huddled against dirty, white-tiled walls, some of the men shoeless, some missing toes; the recurring smell of urine in stairways, and the periodic flickering of lights inside trains when they rounded curves. I tell this story to others and they are appalled that my parents allowed me to fend for myself in an environment that, even then, posed lurking dangers. In today's society, they surely would have received a visit from child protective services.

I was lonely and scared riding the subway alone. But at the time, it was my normal. I had no larger perspective that such experiences were unusual or that they might be due to parental neglect. And I never felt brave. For me, the world was simply an unsafe place where a person had to be constantly vigilant, ever on guard.

Two traumatic occurrences in particular stand out from my metropolis immersion. The first happened on December 16, 1960, roughly two weeks after my eighth birthday. I was taking a bus from school to my grandmother's brownstone near the Park Slope neighborhood of Brooklyn, where my parents would later retrieve me. At one point during the ride to my grandmother's, the bus was stopped by a police officer who climbed aboard and told the driver he would need to take a detour. A plane had crashed.

Later, after arriving at my grandmother's house, I learned that two airplanes had collided and crashed, a TWA in Staten Island and a United at the Brooklyn intersection of 7th Avenue and Sterling Street. All told, 128 people on the planes and six people on the ground were killed. One of the passengers of the United plane lived for a short time. Stephen Baltz, an eleven-year-old from Illinois en route to a holiday family gathering in Yonkers, was found alive in a snow bank with sixty-five cents in change in his pocket. He died the next day of pneumonia from inhaling searing jet fuel.

The United crash was a short distance from my grandmother's house and, in the early evening, we walked to the site. In the twilight, in the middle of the jumbled mess of debris, we saw the tail section of the jet illuminated by spotlights, the word "United" clearly visible. That image and the story of Stephen Baltz remain vivid to this day. They were my introduction to the concept of mortality.

I had my own brush with death earlier that year, although I never realized until much later that I could have been killed. Occasionally, my father would ask me to fetch the morning newspaper from a stand across the street from our Lower East side apartment building. One morning, as I was crossing the street, two painters on their way to work pulled out from behind a double-parked car and slammed into me. They would later tell police they didn't see me until the last second. I, meanwhile, never saw their car at all. The impact promptly emptied my bladder and knocked me to the pavement. I was more frightened than hurt and I never felt pain. Still, the painters insisted that I be taken to a hospital.

A man named Joe, who could often be found standing outside a corner grocery scanning the neighborhood and who I later learned was probably a mob street soldier, notified my parents. The painters, meanwhile, transported me to a hospital where, despite the absence of any external injuries, I was kept for a week, apparently for observation. Something about chemical imbalances, maybe internal injuries.

During my stay at the hospital, I was happily oblivious to all manner of testing and probing because I got to make friends with other children on the floor—no small thing for an only child—and I got to watch television. A lot. That was an even bigger deal. We didn't have a TV in our apartment, owing to my parents' belief that television damaged the mind irreparably. They finally, and much to my relief, relented when I was thirteen, but they never refrained from calling it the "boob tube." Books and carefully crafted words and phrases were their harbors of enlightenment, which were reflected in the clever salutations and closings they used for each other in decidedly unromantic letters ("Pollywog" and "Scallywag" or "Cephus" and "Cassiopeis") and in their infuriating propensity to meticulously articulate words. They never softened a "t" or slurred an "s." And they never swore, unless one counts my mother's exclamations of "fooey" and "hell's bells."

The plane crash and car encounter aside, there were other harrowing big-city experiences. A man tried to kidnap a young girl from the park across the street from our Knickerbocker Village apartment. Two men came to her rescue and pummeled the would-be kidnapper, leaving him bloodied and dazed and lying against the tire of a parked car. I stood there watching as the police hauled him away. Another time, two ships, a freighter and a tanker, collided on the East River under the Manhattan Bridge. The resulting fire lit up the night sky and the ceiling of our apartment. I slept through the commotion, but in the morning I saw the bow of one of the ships sticking out of the water and scampered to my parents' bedroom to tell them a ship was sinking. They already knew. My journalist father had gone down to the river to cover the story for the newspaper.

Occasionally, gangs of teens, benign by today's standards, would encircle younger boys and threaten, in profanity-laced narratives, to do all sorts of horrible-sounding things to them. Toss their hats in dog droppings. Play mumblety-peg with their fingers. Or tie them up to fencing. Every time I was taunted by the hooligans, my heart raced and my face flushed as I searched for a way out. Escape usually meant talking fast, running fast, or both.

Unknown to me at the time, Knickerbocker Village was also purportedly home to a cast of famous and infamous characters, including members of the Bonanno Crime Family, one of the five major organized crime syndicates in New York City. Julius and Ethel Rosenberg, meanwhile, lived in a Knickerbocker Village apartment before they were convicted and later executed at the Sing Sing prison in Ossining, New York, for spying for the Soviet Union.

All this is not to say that living in Knickerbocker Village was a bad thing. I learned to ride a bike on the sidewalks outside the apartments. I spent many wonderful hours playing ball in the park across the street. And for the most part, dangers notwithstanding, I enjoyed the freedom of being able to discover Manhattan and Brooklyn on my own, including spending time at the home of my best friend, Reggie, and his family in Brooklyn. He was black and I was white, but we didn't care about skin color. His friendship and the nurturing nature of his parents instilled in me that pure human goodness and connection were possible.

I didn't care then about being adopted, something I'd always known about myself. I didn't spend a minute wondering about my biological origins, at least not for the first fourteen or so years of my life. I didn't ask adoption-related questions of my parents. And my fantasy about a traveling mother was many years away from taking hold.

In my adolescence, I was simply too busy trying to navigate—and survive—the world around me.

Chapter Three

A copy of a eulogy read at Barbara May Shinn's 2005 funeral arrived via email shortly after the photos, again courtesy of her niece, Carol.

Some of the information I had already gathered, some was new. But one important thing the eulogy underscored was Barbara May's love for animals growing up on the Jersey Shore. The eulogy, delivered by Barbara May's older sister, Nancy, read in part:

> Barbara's love for animals started when she was a small child. Often our mother would say, "I wonder what kind of sick or hurt animal Barbara will bring home today" to love, nurture and nurse back to health. Our home hosted an endless parade of dogs, cats, birds, chicks, pigs and ducks. Her love of animals was passed down to her children.

Perhaps even passed down not just to the children she raised, but also to me through genetic hardwiring. The science is not clear on what personality traits are inherited and what traits result from how a child is nurtured. Any personality similarity between a mother and child who, for instance, might have been separated at birth or shortly thereafter could be nothing more than coincidence. But it could also be the result of a biochemical convergence that researchers haven't yet fully unwrapped.

Whatever the case, nurturing animals—wild and domestic—was at the core of my youth and is still important to me. For much of my childhood, animals served as a balm against a creeping loneliness that was compounded by a splintered marriage between my adoptive mother and father that grew worse as the years passed.

My adoptive mother was a cat lover who for many years bred Siamese, and I was perpetually surrounded by felines and the countless litters they produced. My parents had also purchased fourteen acres of heavily wooded land in Pound Ridge, New York in 1952, before I was adopted and before the Westchester County haven was discovered by a raft of actors, theater producers, writers, and artists. My parents' intent was to build a house, bit by bit, on the rocky, rooted, and often damp property. So, on weekends and sometimes longer during the summers, we'd travel the roughly fifty miles in a stick-shift Plymouth from Manhattan to the Old Mill River Road building site. And it was there amidst the mountain laurel, evergreens, and stately oaks that I traded the frenzied drumbeat of the city for the unhurried hum of the country, discovering nature's wildness in virtually every form.

White-tail deer nestled in patches of tall grasses; snakes, lizards, and chipmunks slipped in and out of large rock piles; crows, jays, chickadees, nuthatches, sparrows, cardinals, orioles, and bluebirds winged through the leafy forest canopy and orchestrally welcomed the sunrises; and possums, raccoons, flying squirrels, and owls ruled the coal-black nights. There were also all manner of pesky insects: mosquitoes, yellow jackets, spiders, horse flies, Japanese beetles, and tent caterpillars among them.

In the first few years while the house was being built, we spent our weekend and summer sojourns to the country in a bulky, weathered Army tent with barely enough room for the three of us and our two cats that accompanied us on the trips. Our bathroom was the forest. Our water supply came from a large, spigoted Army water bag. Meals were cereal in the mornings, liverwurst, peanut butter and jelly or bologna sandwiches at midday, and occasionally freshly caught fish in the evenings. Both the tent and the water bag were likely purchased by my adoptive father from a discount merchant in Lower Manhattan. My father had, after all, served in the Navy, not the Army.

Oddly, my father, a native of Brooklyn and admirer of the city, seemed to take to the primitive life much better than my mother, who was raised on a farm in Sunbury, Ohio, and whose job as a child was to tend to the chickens. One of her biggest peeves was the cats' propensity to leave dead mice in the shoes beside our cots. That and the poison ivy and insect bites. My father, meanwhile, pooh-poohed such country living inconveniences and relished taking bath-showers beneath the water bag.

Progress on the house—a concrete-block structure with enormous picture windows in the butterfly-roofed living room—was slow, either from lack of money or a frugality that led to hiring the cheapest, least efficient labor. We wound up doing a good deal of the work ourselves.

When I wasn't helping build the house, which at one point included gathering and depositing rocks in the spaces between the seventeen-foot-tall chimney flues and the chimney walls, I explored the woods for hours on end. I snacked on wild berries, turned over rocks in search of salamanders, captured hog-nosed, garter and black snakes and brought them back to torment my mother, and delighted in the curiosity of dragonflies. I fished too, bamboo pole in one hand and a can of fat night crawlers in the other, in the rivers, streams, ponds, and reservoirs that surrounded our property.

As time went on—before and after we moved into the still-incomplete country house in 1961 after I finished up the third grade—I began rescuing wild animals. Those that survived I released. Those that died had a place in a makeshift cemetery near a tool shed behind our house. I buried them under discarded chunks of chiseled marble my father had purchased at a bargain-basement price from a bank demolition project in the city. The good pieces became the floor of our living room.

Among the animals in that graveyard was a large orange and white cat I discovered in the woods wedged at the torso in the fork of a tree. The cat was severely dehydrated and barely alive. It died a day later. Another unfortunate animal was a baby weasel that had been left one cold, rainy night in our front yard, either by its mother or a predator. At first, the weasel, which had no visible external injuries, appeared lifeless. But as I held it in my hands, its chest began rising and falling and the weasel started wheezing. I built an incubator to keep the weasel warm and tried giving it milk through an eyedropper. The weasel gradually gained strength and eventually was able to partially raise itself up on its front legs. Then, as suddenly as it had come to life, it died, probably of pneumonia.

People in and around Pound Ridge learned, I guess by word of mouth, about my affection for animals and began bringing me injured or orphaned animals to care for or save. One success story was an orphaned flying squirrel that loved to sit on my shoulder and glide from various perches in my bedroom. I was able to release it after several months. Another success was an orphaned opossum, whose decidedly unpleasant disposition, sharp teeth, and foul odor hastened his release.

One resident brought me three abandoned baby rabbits that had become infested with burrowing maggots. It was almost impossible to extract the maggots and it became clear I would have to euthanize the rabbits. The question was: How? I wanted to be as merciful as possible and I recalled an experience I'd had during an elementary school field trip to Washington, D.C. I still hadn't learned to swim, but I had accepted a dare from several male classmates that I jump off the high dive at the deep end of a motel pool. Better that, I thought at the time, than being taunted, embarrassed, and rejected.

"How come you're swimming in the shallow end with your feet touching the bottom?" one of the boys had asked.

"My feet were not touching the bottom," I'd said, feeling a rush of blood to my face.

"Yes, they were. I saw them. Bet you can't swim."

"Can too."

"Prove it. Dive off the board," the meanest of the boys had said, pointing to the deep end.

"Okay," I'd replied, trying mightily to project fearlessness. "I'll show you."

I marched briskly to the other end of the pool, walked the plank without thinking about much of anything, jumped and hit the water feet first, panicked, flailed to reach the surface, gasped for air and inhaled water, then slowly drifted toward the bottom. On my way down, I felt the hands and arms of someone—a lifeguard, it turned out—lift me quickly to safety. I remembered later that in the moments immediately before my water rescue, when I began slipping into unconsciousness, a comforting peace had enveloped me. It would not have been a bad way to die.

That thought was with me when I got a bucket, filled it with water and held down the first rabbit until it expired. In doing so, I learned something important. The maggots began exiting their holes once they were immersed in water. So, I identified the healthier of the remaining two rabbits and held various parts of the rabbit underwater until the maggots began appearing, allowing me to pluck them out with tweezers. The rabbit lived for a day or two but was too badly wounded to survive. I was crushed. I had done my best and it hadn't been enough.

Still, tending to animals filled the empty spaces in my young life and perhaps it served the same purpose for Barbara May. Her older sister, Nancy, told Carol about the time Barbara May and her son, Eddie, rescued an injured bird. Eddie brought the bird home and mother and son made a splint for its broken wing. When the bird was deemed healed, a ceremony was held to let the bird free.

That benevolent act was part of Barbara May's lifelong affection for animals. She had a hard time containing her excitement about animals when she wrote a letter to her grandmother in October 1940 about a school field trip to a zoo. Barbara May was eight and her cursive was tidy, but her punctuation and capitalization were woefully inconsistent:

Dear grandma:

I was glad to get the letter from you and I hope you are not sick any more I am back to school and so far I have not missed any days Nancy was home from school for a week but she is back to school again. To day our class at school took a trip to Lakewood to see some animals We went in one of the school buses and we had a lot of fun The animals we saw were Red fox squirrl Gray squirrel Flying squirrl Rabbits skunk Pigeons Turkey Peacock canaries Parakeet Pheasant swan Geese Ducks monkey Face owl Red fox Gray fox Racoons and Finches

It has been a long time since I saw you. But I hope I'll see you soon again. Howard is getting to be a big boy now and he is a very good boy

Love Barbara

I don't know if Barbara May was also surrounded by domestic animals, but I was and it was not just the steady procession of cats. Shortly after we moved to the country, my adoptive mother purchased a rather scattered-brained female Airedale, mated it, and that led to a litter of six puppies. She allowed me to keep one of the puppies and I choose the friendliest of the lot and promptly named him Bach, after the famous German composer. Bach, amiable and loyal to a fault, became the best friend I could have. He accompanied me on all of my deep-woods excursions, scampering across the thick bed of brown leaves that blanketed the forest floor and hurdling fallen timbers. He lay down with me in a fort I had built using boulders from the stone walls that meandered through the property, left there by the region's early settlers. He ran alongside me as I zipped down perilously steep, homemade toboggan runs. He slept with me in my bed every night.

Of all the animal deaths I've witnessed or known about, Bach's was the hardest, even though I was twenty-six and nine years gone from Pound Ridge when my mother had him put to sleep. He had kidney problems, arthritis and was, apparently, just plain worn out. My adoptive mother wrote in her diary—a collection of hundreds of eight-by-eleven typed pages—about her decision to euthanize Bach. Her account is tinged with pain, both for Bach's fate and for the fate of her failing marriage:

> I thought it was a purely rational decision and was surprised to find my voice trembling as I talked about it (in a phone call with the veterinarian.) I couldn't bear the thought of trying to get him into the doctor's office for the final step—and the vet agreed to come out to administer the shot. I had spoken to Larry about it last night and again this morning; his only comment was that we might wait a couple of days. I tried to call Larry at the paper, but he wasn't there. He came home, however, before the vet came and was most unsympathetic. "Your decision," he said. "Do what you want to do." I would have liked Bach to live forever. (Bach) couldn't stand up, but he lifted his head and wagged his tail at the vet. The vet administered the shot and in a minute or so he was dead.

That was Bach. Friendly and trusting to the end. He was the one shining example of love in my childhood, my mother notwithstanding. I imagine he occupied the same place in my mother's heart.

Before old age took him, my mother wrote a poem entitled "Walking with Bach" in which she described a triumphant winter trek in the woods with Bach and a new kitten and marked the passage of time. It is one of the few times her prose didn't have undertones of melancholy. It read in part:

> This walk, familiar, is peopled with ghosts,
> Another cat, a child now six-feet-three,
> Could the spring have been greener then?
> Were those October leaves, blinding golds and reds, more crisp?
> The wood smoke sharper?
> I don't believe it.
> Bach has no use for memory; mine plays tricks.
> This is the whitest snow, the highest hill, the longest path.
> We are alive.

Walks with Bach in the untamed landscape my mother had eventually grown to embrace were especially important to her after I left home for college in Bozeman, Montana at seventeen and she was alone with my father's narcissistic mean-spiritedness. That's my term for it. There was likely more to his pathology, but the long and short of it was he constantly put down the people closest to him or ignored them altogether, belittling with an ever-present smirk. He was openly and brazenly bigoted toward anyone who was different from him, including blacks, Jewish people, Catholics, and ignorant souls, the latter who included, in his estimation, almost everyone except for himself.

My adoptive father was emotionally abusive and, for a time, physically abusive to me. One day, when I was fourteen, my father broke my hand with the swift rap of a thick, wooden rake handle. I can't remember what I did that day to anger him; it is obscured by the trauma of the punishment. It's likely I had mouthed off to him about something.

Usually, my father used a wooden yardstick to punish me, and the pattern was always the same. He would summon me ("Come here, Ricky"), I would comply, and my mother would disappear to another room. We would shrink to his demands, even though I was then an inch or so taller than his five-foot-ten and my mother, at five-foot-seven, was very likely physically stronger than him, owing to the farm work she had done growing up.

Yardsticks sting. Rake handles flat-out hurt. And on the day of the hand-breaking, my father couldn't find a yardstick and instead retrieved the rake handle from our utility room and began swinging away at my buttocks while I was pressed stomach-first against a kitchen counter. I instinctively tried to block the blows with my left hand and felt a searing heat when the rake handle hit the metacarpal bone leading to the pinky. The swelling was instantaneous.

My mother treated the nasty-looking hump by soaking my hand in Epsom salts. We all then went about our business as if nothing had happened, even though my hand seemed permanently swollen. The inaction, I think, stemmed from my adoptive parents' belief that people should go to the doctor only if they were near death. I think, but I don't know for sure, they were also horrified about the incident.

My father didn't voice any regret. Perhaps I am giving him the benefit of the doubt that his silence after the beating was evidence of concern. My mother, meanwhile, periodically asked in gentle tones how my hand was feeling.

One week later, my mother, realizing I might have a serious injury, took me to our family physician. She instructed me to tell the doctor I'd injured my hand in an accidental fall and I complied. X-rays ultimately revealed a clear break that had already begun to heal improperly, and the doctor, without warning, re-broke the bone with his bare hands and set it. From that day on, I understood that the real reason for the broken bone would remain a family secret.

It wasn't the first time my mother, loving as she was to me, ineptly tried to keep the peace by covering up my father's abuse. It wasn't the last time my father's ill temper would surface. I had hoped the whole rake incident might prompt him to change his ways. It didn't.

In my time living with my adoptive mother and father, my father never told me or my mother he loved us or was proud of us. I never saw my parents hug, kiss, or hold hands. By the time I was in high school, my parents were sleeping in separate bedrooms. Neither my mother nor me ever heard an encouraging word from my father, and often we faced crude, blistering commentary from him.

One day in particular stands out. I was a teenager and my father was upset about something I'd done; again, I don't remember what it was. I hurried to my bedroom and shut the door to escape what surely would be a spray of angry, disparaging words directed toward me. Even that maneuver, though, didn't spare me. As my father plodded down the hallway of our Pound Ridge home, his ratty slippers slapping against the concrete floor, he said loudly:

"Insolent child, Betty. We never should have adopted him."

"Stop it, Larry," my mother scolded from the living room.

"Miserable world," he muttered. "Miserable world."

"If you know of a better one, Larry, why don't you go to it," my mother shot back.

Such was the toxic environment in our home. I learned to numb myself against it, but the emotional and physical abuse took an enormous toll on me, something I wouldn't realize until I became an adult.

Only once did I respond violently to my adoptive father's abuse. I pushed him down into a thorny bed of roses after he harangued me about not doing my chores. I felt momentary satisfaction, then guilt and depression. A truly good boy should tolerate his father's moods.

The consuming cheerlessness of our home devastated my mother too, although I wouldn't know the extent of it until after her death from cancer in 1994 at the age of seventy-six. Her anguish spilled out in the diary she left behind, in the poems she wrote, and in the copies of letters she sent to Larry when he was out of town. She blamed her bad marriage on herself, regretted with profound guilt that she hadn't done more to protect me from my father, and thought about ending her life more than once. Her private sadness was ever-present.

She usually wore a smile and almost always had a kind, thoughtful word for others. But beneath that façade lurked a deep insecurity about her worth as a mother and as a wife, even though she worked hard to shed her by-the-book pragmatism and be nurturing and compassionate toward my father and me. She constantly tried to become a better person and she was exceedingly bright. She was a far better writer than either my father or me, and she also crafted and edited crossword puzzles, a good number of which were published. She was an adept bridge player, an inspiring teacher, and she was attractive. I thought she looked a little like actress Ava Gardner.

None of her considerable attributes, though, seemed to buoy her, and perhaps it was her lack of self-worth that kept her hopelessly tethered to an utterly dysfunctional marriage. What parts of her remarkable character my father didn't decimate she stripped away herself.

Shortly before Christmas in 1961, her self-criticism revealed itself when she sat down at an old typewriter in the den and listed these perceived personal deficits:

1. The fact that I am not a genius. This acceptance is long overdue.
2. The jobs I didn't take, the paths I didn't travel.
3. The fact that I'm not clever, witty, brilliant.
4. The fact that I'm not the most beautiful woman in the world. Hardly anyone is. Try to be neat and clean.
5. The fact that I'm not the most popular woman in the room. Instead, be pleasant to all the others who aren't too.
6. Our lack of children. (They couldn't be nicer than Ricky.)
7. Bad luck. It could have been worse, and we've had more than our share of good.
8. Mistakes. Just try not to make the same one again.
9. Larry's shortcomings. Instead, learn to live with them, and try to improve my own.
10. How childish this all is, and the fact that I've tried it many times before. Maybe this time it will work.

She went on to resolve to compare herself not with the best but with the mediocre and reminded herself that, at least from her perspective, she was responsible for family harmony. She was forty-three years old the day she relegated herself to a low bar. Two years later, while she and I traveled to the grocery store and in a brief burst of self-confidence, she turned to me from the driver's seat and asked what I would think about the idea of "your father and I" getting a divorce. "That would be great," I said. I would finally escape the torment of my disapproving father, and my mother and I would live happily ever after. I was eleven years old that day. The topic was never discussed again and the divorce never happened.

Until I read her diary, I was unaware of the depths of her internal discontent. I never realized I was the reason she got up in the morning or that I may have been one of the few things she believed she got right in her life. I also never realized she probably could have, in fact, done more to shield me from my father, even though she was extraordinarily loving and supportive. She often addressed me as "Richard, honey" or "Richard, dear." And she told me more than once that she loved me and was proud of me. But she also at times seemed to watch the chasm between me and my father from a distance and assess, in an academic way, how well I was handling it. She wrote about it occasionally more as a disconnected observer than a vital family participant—a revelation that disturbed me and explained, at least in part, my feelings of insecurity growing up. It had always been hard for me to be angry with her, but I was indeed angry after reading her diary. I understood, for the first time, why I had felt so trapped in my childhood, so lacking a safe space, so confused about what love was. My mother had committed to living with my father's shortcomings and in turn had required that I suffer through them too. She defended him even when he didn't merit defense.

Once, after my father had chastised me for doing poorly in school and I complained to my mother that he didn't love me, she said, "Your father *does* love you."

"Then why won't he tell me?" I asked.

"Because he doesn't know how."

It was an unacceptable answer to me then, but it did seem to be the case. He had an innate inability to love and the ways in which he tried to show affection for me were sadly twisted. When he visited me in the intensive care unit after I was hit by the car, he brought my schoolbooks. I think that signified both his hope I would survive and his need to make sure that I kept up with my homework. My father's conception of what a child should be doing always revolved around some form of work, and hardly a week passed when he didn't demand that I spend my idle hours cutting the thick stands of brush that surrounded our Pound Ridge property.

Even when he tried to take an interest in my interests, he misfired. He once volunteered to coach a lower level Little League team, even though he knew little about baseball and had only played catch with me once or twice. I, meanwhile, was on the major league team and so, on the days when both teams practiced, I played on the regular field and periodically watched him coach other kids on the grass beyond the chain-link centerfield fence. He just never seemed able to get close to me.

Of all the baseball games I played in through the age of sixteen, my father attended just one, and he brought along a business acquaintance, perhaps to show that he was a caring father. I pitched my heart out that day, hoping he'd offer a kind word or a pat on the back. I received neither. To this day, I can't watch the scene from the movie *Field of Dreams*—the one in which the son asks the father if he wants to have a catch—without crying. I made darn sure to play catch as often as possible with two of my sons who were interested in baseball.

The only thing I can remember doing that demonstrably pleased my father was bringing home the bass, perch, trout, and bluegill I caught in nearby waterways. I'd gut, scale, and filet them and my father would fry them in butter. "Good fish, Ricky," he would say.

I brought lots of fish home in my youth.

Over the years, my mother increasingly excused my father's behavior toward me, ascribing it to his own ill-tempered, aloof father or to professional disappointments, including the demise of the *World-Telegram & Sun* in 1966.

My father had landed quickly at the *New York World Journal Tribune* after the *Telegram & Sun* folded. His new place of employment was a Hail Mary merger designed to save three papers: The *Telegram & Sun*, the *New York Journal American* and the *New York Herald Tribune*. But it lasted just ten months, my father left the business entirely to become a college logic professor, and his mood seemed to grow ever darker after that.

My mother escaped the pervasive gloom of our lives by downing glasses of brandy and wine or by retreating to the bathroom, where she spent hours chain-smoking cigarettes and doing crossword puzzles. "Be out in a minute," she would say when someone knocked. But it was never just one minute. It was always a long series of minutes. The air in the bathroom was barely breathable when she was done.

She also spent hours working in her flower gardens, ascending to near euphoria whenever she spotted a bluebird. "Oh look!" she would exclaim if I happened to be nearby. "It's a bluebird. How marvelous." For her, bluebirds seemed to be a calming, albeit elusive, remedy for her sadness.

My father's retreat was the den, where he would sit puffing on a pipe, strands of uncombed, graying hair feathering out from his largely bald head. Some days, he would tap out something on the typewriter, the syncopated clicking permeating the house. Other days, he would harshly critique, with red pen in hand, the latest edition of the *New York Times*. Perhaps that fed his need to position himself as a superior intellect.

I would escape by either disappearing into the woods or secluding myself in my room, where I would invent games one could play alone and at night wait, sometimes for hours, for a calming sleep to come. Nights were the worst, the loneliest. The thick woods around the house obscured any light that might come from the occasional traffic below our winding six hundred-foot-long driveway or from neighboring houses, which were a good distance away. Sometimes the woods would even blot out the moon.

Many nights, I lay awake on the bed in my room staring at the blackness beyond the windows and listening to the cacophony of crickets, cicadas, tree frogs, owls, and other sounds I could not identify. And in the din of the darkness, I felt terminally without hope.

My mother kept me company when she could and we spent many wonderful hours playing Scrabble, which much to her dismay I began mastering. She simply hated to lose when it came to matters of the mind, although sometimes she sabotaged herself by delighting in forming obscure words rather than scoring points. I simply liked to win whenever I could because most of the time I felt like I was on the losing end of things.

As fun and bonding as the Scrabble sessions were, I think my mother also viewed them as strategic opportunities to educate me—to expose me to a challenging level of intellectual pursuit. She was less successful in introducing me to classical music by way of piano lessons, which seemed more like homework than an exciting learning experience. Our old, upright piano was out of tune, and my parents' reminders that I practice sounded punitive. I had also gravitated to folk, pop, and rock as my choices for musical enjoyment and eventually took up the guitar. Classical music then, and to a certain extent now, seemed plodding, unbearably long, and didn't inspire me. Its meandering moodiness seemed to reinforce the unhappiness that consumed our lives.

Relief came for my mother in 1989 when my father suffered a massive heart attack at the age of seventy-five. He rose from the table in the kitchen nook of the Pound Ridge home, keeled over, and likely died before hitting the floor face first. It was, for my mother, a welcome end to a forty-seven-year marriage, and she spent the final five years of her life living on her terms, which included a good deal of domestic and international travel. After she passed at the age of seventy-six, and per her wishes, I spread her ashes on her former family farm in Sunbury, Ohio. I stood alone at one corner of a ploughed field, reflected on our life together, and wished her well in her next chapter. Her ashes fanned out across the rich earth under a moonlit sky.

My father was also freed from his own torment upon his death. In his waning years, he had grown ever more bitter, believing that the world owed him more than he had been given—at least that's the way my mother described it. He had tried to earn a doctorate and failed. His journalism career had been rudely upended. A book he had written about Supreme Court Justice Felix Frankfurter was never published. I believe he also felt that he was stuck with a wife and son who didn't measure up to his standards.

I, meanwhile, remained shackled to his abuse long after his death. It took me many years to stop trying to please a man who could never be pleased. In life, physical and verbal abuse aside, he was often distant and dismissive, even as I grew into adulthood, even as I began my journalism career. In my mid-20s, I asked him once to share what he knew about the profession. His response was, "There's not much to say." I never asked him again.

In my mid-30s, I confronted him about his behavior when my adoptive parents visited me and my wife in Colorado. When my wife, our young son, and my mother went shopping, I launched into a rant. My father was sitting in the kitchen nook of our apartment. I was in the living room. I spent a good twenty minutes pacing and rambling about his beatings, his cruel words, his insensitivity to my feelings, and all the time he hadn't spent with me. I rarely took my eyes off him and chose my words as carefully as I could. When I was done, I waited for a response, and it seemed like forever before he spoke. "I don't know what you're talking about," he finally said. I was speechless. I can't imagine why I was expecting more from him, but I was.

Even in death, he cut me to the quick. At his viewing, I noticed his snide smirk of hubris frozen on his face. The mortician was too adept.

My mother and I did exact some retribution. At my father's funeral, the pastor, who barely knew him, delivered a eulogy based on the recollections of people outside our family who had experienced a slightly more charming side of my father, a side we rarely saw. At one point, the pastor described my father as an "amiable irritant" and my mother and I looked at each other, decided it was an apt description of his public persona, and she later had the words etched in his gravestone. Self-centered as he was, my father would have loved it.

Barbara May's relatives recounted that she, her older sister Nancy, and younger brother Howard, may have also experienced a difficult relationship with their father, Harold, especially after their mother, Florence, died in 1945 at the age of thirty-nine from heart-related complications stemming from rheumatic fever. Barbara May was thirteen, Nancy was fifteen, and Howard was seven when their mother died. Their father, relatives said, drank heavily and was not a particularly nice man. The three children sought comfort from others in the extended family, especially an aunt, Anastasia. All three were eager to leave home once they were old enough.

I, too, had wonderful relatives—and a few close friends—and when I spent time in their homes, I felt as though I was getting a glimpse of what a family environment should be: stable, loving and nurturing. I especially enjoyed trips to Ohio to visit cousins and other relatives on my mother's side. Later, some of those cousins moved close to us in New York, and that provided another escape from my gloom.

The relatives on my mother's side treated me as they would have treated a biological relative. Aunts and uncles always remembered me on my birthdays and at Christmas. And when we visited the New York relatives in Shrub Oak, an older cousin and I spent hours in the lower level of the house drinking Coke and playing ping pong, floor hockey, and the sports board games Pigskin and Strato-O-Matic.

But internally, starting in my early teens, there was a part of me that felt like an outsider in the homes of relatives. For periods of time, I could pretend that I was part of the relatives' families and revel in the joy of being around seemingly happy people. But after every visit, the awareness that I was not really related to them emerged on the drive back to Pound Ridge. I sat in the back seat and listened to my parents bicker—about my father's driving ("Larry, stay on your side of the road.") or my mother's interpretation of a discussion the adults had had earlier in the evening ("Betty, you don't know what you're talking about."). And in those unpleasant moments, I was left emotionally stranded between the place I preferred to be—with my relatives—and the place I loathed. Neither place, though, was home and it wasn't just about buildings or geography. It was about lacking a home in the figurative sense, a place of belonging.

So, I too couldn't wait to flee when I was old enough, to find "home," to break free from a father marinated in hate, and to escape the trappings of a largely affluent area that struck me as unfriendly, pretentious, and disingenuous.

Pound Ridge between the mid to late 1960s, my middle and high school years, was a town of about 3,700 people with narrow, hilly, winding country roads. Residents generally owned large parcels of land and their homes, sometimes hidden from view by dense curtains of trees and shrubs, reflected a wide variety of architecture, some of it dating to the late eighteenth century.

The main business district in Pound Ridge was Scotts Corners, a short stretch of road with a grocery and sundry retail shops. People could also shop in the other little New York towns around Pound Ridge—Bedford Village, Bedford Hills, and the larger Mount Kisco—or travel to nearby New Canaan or Stamford, Connecticut.

There were people who lived at the cliff's edge of sustainability in Pound Ridge and the surrounding towns, but affluence was the norm. There were business professionals who worked in New York City and commuted by car or train. There were entertainers, artists, television pioneers, and writers of note, and there were the privileged sons and daughters of the elite who seemed to have everything. Then there was me. Lucky if I got two pairs of pants from Sears at Christmas. Despondent about my home life. A below-average student. Unsure if I could ever measure up to anybody.

Susan Dey was in my homeroom at Fox Lane High School until her senior year, when she left to play Laurie Partridge on the sitcom "The Partridge Family." Hilary Cosell, daughter of famed sportscaster Howard Cosell, attended Pound Ridge Elementary and then Fox Lane when I attended both schools. Mark and Richard Hunter, sons of writer Evan Hunter, best known for his "87th Precinct" crime novels written under the pen name Ed McBain, were also classmates of mine. The son of Lucile and William Baring-Gould, authors of the acclaimed "The Annotated Mother Goose," attended Fox Lane a few years ahead of me.

Before, during, or after my time in Pound Ridge, there were others. Actors Hume Cronyn and Jessica Tandy attended the church where I was confirmed, actress Susan Sarandon volunteered at the Pound Ridge Library where my mother was also a volunteer, and actress Ali MacGraw was born in Pound Ridge. The list is long of notable Pound Ridgers past and present: Richard Gere; Christopher and Dana Reeve; Eli Wallach; Eartha Kitt; Tom Brokaw; Tallulah Bankhead; Fred Gwynne, and Vera Wang, among them. Muppet creator Jim Henson lived one town over in Bedford Village. President Bill Clinton and former Secretary of State Hillary Clinton moved into a home in Chappaqua, a town I represented as a teenage amateur ice hockey player.

My mother and father also had among their friends the famous and almost famous. Noted mystery writer Evelyn Smith, best known for her "Miss Melville" series, was a close family friend. So was Ed Spingarn, who dreamed of being a great writer but, to the best of my recollection, produced exactly one published book, "*Perfect 36,*" a paperback novel described on the cover as "a revealing and riotous story of the bosom business." Both of them lived in New York City, but they kept in touch after we moved to Westchester County.

As a pre-teen and teenager in Pound Ridge, I felt as if we were poorer than everyone else, that all of my classmates were smarter than me, and that many of my peers seemed to move through their formative years with an air of conceit and entitlement. My sagging self-esteem—a condition I blame squarely on my adoptive father—likely contributed to this impression.

The truth is, we weren't poor. I learned this later in my travels when I saw the dilapidated shacks in the hills and hollers of eastern Kentucky and the life-worn faces of the inhabitants, the rusted-out mobile homes along forgotten two-lane highways in America's heartland, and the peeling-paint, broken-windowed hovels in the shadows of the nation's urban centers. The truth is, I wasn't dumb either. Not brilliant. But not completely lacking in intelligence.

Nevertheless, just as I never felt truly connected to family growing up, I never felt welcome in my schools or community. I was a cast-out child of the world, free to wander and explore. Abandoned by my birth mother and father and then abandoned again by an adoptive father who didn't know how to love, and to a lesser degree by an adoptive mother who was caught up in the struggle of trying to rescue three people: her husband, her son, and herself.

Animals, then, became my sanctuary, a haven that I turned to when seeking true acceptance and where I was removed from the specter of human cruelty. Throughout my high school years, I worked at a kennel in nearby Vista, New York, that was owned by a caring family man and managed by a heavily accented immigrant from Denmark who was forever extolling the nutritional value of cheese.

I fed the boarded animals, cleaned the cages and runs, shampooed dogs, and clipped nails. It was one of several jobs I had while in high school. I also worked at an upscale restaurant in Pound Ridge called Emily Shaw's, where I cut bread, prepared chocolate mousses, delivered relish trays and parked the expensive cars, many of them fancy imports, belonging to the diners. The valet tips were exceptional, especially for a high schooler.

I returned to formalized animal care many years later when I volunteered with a raptor rehabilitation organization in Indiana, helping heal injured or ill birds of prey and returning them to the wild, and giving educational presentations. Among the birds were Red-Tailed Hawks, Great Horned Owls, Screech Owls, Barred Owls, Cooper's Hawks, and Kestrels. Some of them angry. Some of them timid. Some of them trusting and loving. All of them simultaneously lethal and yet representative of the beauty of nature's designs.

For the past twenty years or so, I have also fed and communed with the racoons and possums that have ventured into the backyards of homes where I've lived. Not one has acted in a threatening fashion, and some have become quite friendly.

To gain the trust of a wild animal, to look deeply into the golden eyes of a Great Horned Owl perched on the hand, to feel the rhythmic purring of a cat against the chest, to take a long walk in the woods with a dog, to delight in the release of an animal once ill or injured—these moments bind my heart and soul with another's in a way no other relationship can.

I imagine Barbara May discovered, as I have, that the animal world is far less complicated and far more forgiving than the world of humans, and if one earnestly takes the time to develop relationships with animals, the rules of give and take are consistent and largely predictable. Any love shown is unconditional, save for the expectation to be fed; the allegiances of animals are void of human-perfected strategies of manipulation and deception; and animals listen without judgment.

Animals, once befriended and understood, simply don't have perplexing agendas, and this makes them safer and easier for me to embrace—especially when the world around me has been, for most of my life, filled with crosscurrents of discord.

Chapter Four

My tumultuous childhood did not influence any searches I conducted for my birth mother—at least not consciously. Most of the time, any searching I did was borne of sporadic spurts of natural curiosity.

Although I'd often wondered who my birth mother might be, I made a decision in my late teens that I would largely refrain from looking for her, and only then in limited ways with little follow-up. I felt it important to form my own identity independent of any distracting information that might arise from knowing about my biological origins. I was worried that whatever I found out about my mother, especially if it was unflattering, would feed my insecurities.

I also didn't want to be that dark secret that showed up on someone's doorstep and upended their life and the lives of those around them, and I was afraid of being rejected, especially in a life filled with its fair share of rejection and abandonment. As much as I yearned at times to meet my birth mother, to express my gratitude to her, it would've been devastating to be turned away by her twice.

The fear of rejection and abandonment, real and pervasive in other areas of my life, was as much a result of life experiences as it was an apparently inherent lack of self-worth. And one thing that reinforced my unworthiness was my pathetic academic performance in school. I was unable to see the relevance of most lessons. More problematic was that I was unable to concentrate for any length of time, even on the topics that might have triggered my interest. My brain could not land firmly on a direction or concept for more than a few seconds or minutes.

Today, I imagine, I might have been diagnosed with ADHD or worse. Borrowing from the title of a book by Kay Redfield Jamison, I had "an unquiet mind."

Against the backdrop of unfocused thinking was the fact that the vast majority of my cousins, especially on my mother's side, were maddeningly brilliant. Their academic successes became a painful standard to which I was frequently compared, especially by my father. Worse, because of the dysfunction between my adoptive mother and father, I had no clue what it meant to be a boy or a man or a friend or a lover. That left me susceptible to ridicule by mean-spirited peers—something I endured periodically throughout my young life—because I had no well of confidence from which to draw. I was a hopeless, introverted mishmash of incongruent parts.

One experience in the third grade, while it might have fortified anyone else, did nothing to enhance my self-esteem. The private school I attended had scheduled a father-son day in which the boys would square off against each other in short, gloved boxing matches on the gym floor. A boy named Peter, who had been incessantly harassing me verbally, challenged me to a match and I accepted, fearful that declining his challenge would only worsen the bullying. Although I was quite certain he would beat me to a pulp, I caught him flush on the chin at one point and dropped him. I can still see the startled look in his eyes as he lay on his back looking up at me. He never bothered me again, but I considered it a lucky punch and in no way evidence of either my physical or emotional strength.

Still, animal encounters notwithstanding, one of the only places where I felt worthwhile was in sporting activities, where the modicum of success I achieved kept me staggering forward. I played baseball with a good arm and no bat in Little League and Babe Ruth League, the arm cultivated early on by throwing tennis balls against the wall in that New York City park and rocks against a giant oak at the foot of our driveway in Pound Ridge. I was also a better-than-average ice hockey goalie who went from weekend pond hockey outings to helping the Chappaqua Flyers in Westchester County win an amateur league championship in my senior year of high school. I played a fair game of lacrosse as the goalie at Fox Lane High School, where I was given the starting nod, even though I had never played the sport before, based solely on my ice hockey prowess. I also competed in high school track and cross country, occasionally winning medals in the triple jump and the 220- and 440-yard events, before those races were converted to meters.

I enjoyed being the center of attention as a pitcher and goalie, and found that in those two positions I could achieve a measure of control that I lacked in almost every other aspect of my life. More than that, I was drawn to the warrior spirit needed to confront sporting rivals who intended to do a person harm. It was a "me vs. them" thing. I reveled in keeping batters off the bases and shooters out of the net, and if I had been any better at either skill I might have chosen one for a career. But batters began catching up to my fastballs. And, when my best friend since the fourth grade, J.C. Perkins, and I attended a hockey camp run by NHL'ers in New Hyde Park, Long Island, in the summer of 1969—in the same week that man landed on the moon—I discovered I was no match for the blistering blue-line slap shots of New York Rangers legends Rod Gilbert and Brad Park and the hard, in-close wrist shots of enforcer Reggie Fleming. It's difficult to stop a ninety-plus-miles-per-hour shot when you can't even see the darn thing. But even to stand in net to face speeding frozen missiles was a confidence-builder. So, too, was denying Park on several simulated breakaways.

I was much less successful in cross country, intimidated at the outset by Pound Ridge resident and Fox Lane distance star Dave Pottetti, who was several years older than me. Dave, like me, was an introvert and struggled with socializing. But if people in town didn't know Dave personally, they certainly saw him running fleet-footed along the country-road hills and valleys of Pound Ridge. Even now, when I think of those roads, I think of Dave. I see Dave.

I encountered Dave several times on my training runs and he encouraged me to tag along, but I simply could not keep up. It's no wonder. He had beaten future Olympian Marty Liquori as a prep standout and later, when he attended Harvard, ran admirably against Yale's Frank Shorter, who would win marathon gold in the 1972 Olympics. Dave seemed to have it all: a national reputation as a runner and academic achievement at Harvard. But in the same year Shorter conquered the marathon, Dave died at the age of twenty-two from a self-inflicted gunshot wound. His body was found in a Navajo Hogan he had constructed on his family's Pound Ridge property.

Dave had acknowledged from time to time in news stories that he no longer found joy in running and was intent on developing his inner spiritual self. If his demons were anything like mine, I can relate to his challenges. Nevertheless, when I first heard about his death, I wondered how a person so gifted could throw it all away.

I never seriously considered suicide as an answer to my problems, but to say I was painfully insecure, overly sensitive, and socially awkward before athletics saved me would be an understatement. One incident that stands out was a middle school field trip to the Natural History Museum in New York City. I walked up to a female classmate with jaw-dropping physical attributes and, although I had never spoken to her before, asked her to "go steady." She laughed at me, my face flushed, and I walked away in shame. Fortunately, the only witnesses were her girlfriend and the skeleton of a rather large dinosaur. It was not the first nor would it be the last time that my naïveté would rear up and slap me, especially when it came to girls.

Thank goodness for sports. Ridiculous as it sounds, sports achievements helped mask my interpersonal ineptitude. They elevated my stature in the eyes of my peers and drew the attention of female admirers. And so it was that a few years after that unfortunate middle school misfire, there were a handful of high school girls who attended games and eagerly offered themselves to me and a teammate in post-game make-out sessions, often in the cramped confines of my beloved blue Volkswagen Beetle.

I met my only true girlfriend in high school through sports and fell hard, without walls or caution. I was, after all, still terribly naïve and vulnerable behind my athletic armor. She was only the second girl I had ever chosen to trust. The first was a kind-hearted elementary school classmate named Lucy. I carried Lucy's books to classes, we held hands occasionally, and we kissed—a brief peck on the lips—during a chaperoned party. Within a year of that kiss, she and her family moved to the Midwest and that was that. I don't recall feeling abandoned, but I'm sure I must have.

My high school girlfriend was playful, cute, and short—four-foot-ten—and her bubbly spirit was a marvelous antidote to my home life and low self-esteem. She affectionately called me "bozo" because the hair on the sides of my head would go full-mast in the wind. I called her "squirt." We met during track practice, dated for about six months, and then, without warning, she dumped me during a field trip to hear famed lawyer and civil rights activist William Kunstler deliver a speech on the village green in Bedford Village. I can't remember if she told me or someone else did, but I learned she had become uncomfortable with the growing physical intimacy of our relationship. Several months later at a clandestine gathering of teenagers in the woods, I found her romantically involved with someone I had considered a friend. The devastation of the breakup and the ensuing deception shadowed me for many years, further cementing my fear of abandonment.

As a person already befuddled by so many things, I also wasn't helped by the upheavals of the 1960s: the assassination of President John F. Kennedy in 1963 and the killing of his purported assailant, Lee Harvey Oswald. The race riots. The Vietnam War. The assassinations of Malcom X in 1965 and Bobby Kennedy and Martin Luther King Jr. in 1968. Not to mention the advent of harder-edged, rebellious rock n' roll; readily available, inexpensive mind-altering drugs, and free love that by today's standards would be considered rampant promiscuity. The turmoil in my own home was exceeded only by the caldron of chaos in the world, and it seemed like there was no place where I could center myself.

At no time was I more aware of a world spinning off its axis than when, as a high school sophomore, I attended my first rock concert at the age fifteen—a performance by The Jimi Hendrix Experience at the Westchester County Center in White Plains, New York on April 6, 1968. Marijuana smoke clouded the spaces around us, and the moment Hendrix launched into "Purple Haze" I knew my feeling of being a free-wandering spirit—of being a motherless child, as Richie Havens would put it—would be a part of me for a long, long time. The music of the '60s could have that effect on young people seeking belonging, adopted or not.

Later on and until we graduated high school, J.C. and I traveled to New York City's Filmore East to catch some of the greatest musical acts of the time, including Jefferson Airplane, Led Zeppelin, and Santana. One of the most memorable concerts was a midnight-to-dawn performance by the Grateful Dead and the New Riders of the Purple Sage. It was a long, crazy affair filled with impromptu jamming, acid-fueled dancing (we were among the sober ones) and boisterous sing-alongs. Occasionally, when some members of the Dead took breaks while the rest of the group played, they would sit in the audience and converse with concert-goers. Founding Dead member Ron "Pigpen" McKernan, who would die several years later of a massive drinking-related gastrointestinal hemorrhage, sat several seats away from us. When the concert was over, Jerry Garcia and the boys joined all of us in walking out of the Filmore and into the streets of the East Village, a veritable swarm of merry vagabonds of rebellion.

A short time later, in the fall of 1970 and at the age of seventeen, I would enroll at Montana State University—some 2,200 miles from New York—on the lure of snow-capped mountains, escape from a confusing childhood riddled with self-doubt, and to seize a student deferment and avoid the military draft. The senseless and violent Vietnam War scared me, I would not have made a good soldier, and I was deeply aligned with the peace movement. As I was about to enter my second year of college, the student deferment would become crucial to me: My birth date came up No. 1 in the draft lottery—an ominous sign, to say the least.

I still think I made the right choice to seek a student deferment, although I have occasionally felt guilty that I may have shirked my duty to country by circumventing the draft, even if it was perfectly legal.

I knew little about Montana before arriving in Bozeman other than what I had read in a tourist publication. I had no family ties to the university or the state. I had no idea what I wanted to study or what career I might pursue. All I knew was that Montana State, known then mostly as an agricultural school, wanted me and was offering a ticket to get away. That was enough.

What I discovered in Montana in the early '70s was a last frontier of prairie, wilderness, water, and mountains under a big sky far removed from the fast-paced din of modern civilization. It was a land of real cowboys, cowgirls, rodeos, and well-worn shit-kickers, fine fishing and hunting, spectacular hiking and skiing, and bears, buffalo, elk, bobcats and coyotes. In Montana then, perhaps even now, a person could do and be whatever they wanted—unless that person was Native American. One thing Montana had in common with the rest of the country was racial and cultural discrimination, and I witnessed first-hand a decided detest for "injuns," something I found difficult to stomach. I understood what it felt to be ostracized, as I had been by my father and by a number of my peers.

Some college classmates liberally and dismissively used the word "injun," as in "he's nothing but an injun." Several young white men in my dorm also made an almost weekly habit of taking turns with a young Native American female student—and laughing about the sexual encounters afterward. I watched her walk down the dorm hallway to one of the men's rooms and her expressionless demeanor gave me the impression that she lacked self-worth. I suspected there were others like her and I understand now that Native American students who arrived directly from their homes on the reservations may have been vulnerable to slurs and other forms of abuse due to generational trauma emanating from decades of oppression and marginalization.

There were other reasons Montana took some getting used to, especially for a New Yorker. Cowboys and cowgirls practiced their roping skills on fixed outdoor campus objects, I had never before seen such a preponderance of pickup trucks and gun racks, and many of the MSU students had little awareness of lives lived by others beyond Montana's borders. Moreover, the sheer expansiveness of the horizon created an anxiety in me for at least a year. On the east coast, I was accustomed to trees getting in the way of one's view. In Montana, in Big Sky Country, it seemed like you could see forever.

I was, nevertheless, determined to stick it out. And over time, the pristine, distraction-free isolation of Montana became a perfect place for me to begin to unravel my emotional baggage and try to figure out who I was. It was not an orderly or rational pursuit. In college, I often lived at different extremes simultaneously.

I worked on friends' ranches, bailing hay, bringing cattle in at dusk from high in the saddle, and in our spare time hunting elk with thirty-aught-sixes from the grassy ridges overlooking coulees. Thankfully, my aim was abysmal; I am not fond of killing mammals. I joined the excursions more to experience adventure in the rugged western landscape.

I also grew my hair long and immersed myself in a vibrant drug, party, and concert scene. I saw such performers as The Youngbloods and a barely discovered John Denver in cozy campus music spaces. I skinny-dipped stoned on starry nights at the remote Norris Hot Springs before it was commercialized anew. I smoked pot almost every day and dabbled with mescaline, various forms of acid, and MDA (the love drug). I got hooked on white crosses (speed), which I liberally consumed throughout the day. Most of the drugs I took just to experiment with expanding the horizons of my consciousness. Speed was a different story. Speed energized me and mitigated my introversion. I became gregarious and, from my perspective, interesting to others. I also became stuck in the predictable cycle of pleasant highs and painful lows.

I drifted in and out of organized religion, both cognizant of the value of some Biblical wisdom and disgusted by the frequent hypocrisy that ran counter to the

Biblical warning about focusing on the speck in someone else's eye without seeing the log in yours.

I was one part conservative right-wing pretender, one part leftist hippie, and many parts still undefined. The contemporary term for me might have been "a hot mess."

While I was learning a great deal from exploring life at the edges, my academic showing remained unremarkable, if not embarrassing. I was still having trouble concentrating in class and understanding the relevance of the coursework. I was also prone to jumping into and out of relationships.

For a while, I lived with a girl from Minnesota in a small log cabin on the outskirts of Bozeman with a ramshackle outhouse and no running water. The property owner reduced my rent in return for watching several dozen head of cattle that lived in a fenced field behind the cabin. One night, my girlfriend and I heard what sounded like the pounding of a stampede. When we went outside, we discovered the cows had rammed through the fence and were now standing, all of them, in the middle of the road that ran past the cabin. Cows, I learned, don't respond well to polite verbal commands, especially from a barefoot, half-dressed, half-asleep pioneer wannabe. If it hadn't been for the help of a passing-through rancher and his dog, the cows likely would have been standing there at daybreak.

At another point, I lived in a house in town with four other roommates, all of us cycling through various stages of stoned, and some, myself included, inviting girlfriends to stay overnight. My girlfriend at the time was the daughter of a Montana State dean and he was hardly pleased with our relationship, especially after we announced we were considering marriage. One day, he asked me, "How do you intend to support our daughter in the manner she is accustomed to?" I don't recall my answer, but I do know I had no idea how I was going to support her. In the end, it wouldn't matter. She gave in to parental pressure, broke up with me, and eventually married a man with an aristocratic-sounding name.

For a short time, I lived in a room in the basement of a home owned by a decorated World War II hero, paid thirty-five dollars a month in rent, fixed meals on a hot plate, and took showers from an overhead spigot in the middle of the basement. Later, I spent a couple of months in the home of a troubled Vietnam War veteran who nearly killed himself one night. He had dropped acid and I found him sitting in a chair in the center of the living room staring at a wall. He was holding a gun in his lap. I talked to him for several hours, trying to reach him through the maze of his hallucinations. We made it through the night, but I never knew what became of him after I moved from his house. The experience gave me a first-hand look at the psychological damage done by war—a fate that might have befallen me had I chosen to serve.

Toward the end of my college experience, I lived in a house of Jesus followers and we participated in regular Bible studies—which is not to say we were removed from sin. Sometimes, I simply shacked up for a night or two with the latest woman who was the object of my affection. One of them was an adventurous, older, married woman who paid virtually all of my school and living expenses in return for sexual favors—until the excitement of the risk waned for her, or she simply tired of me. Her come-on line had been, "Stay with me, I'm loaded." She was talking about money. In another escapade, I hung out with a sweet, free-spirited flower child who invited me into her bed every night and brought me rose hip tea in the morning. She loved to cuddle, but insisted we never have sex.

In my youthful dalliances—even in the more serious relationships—I suspect I was looking not only for acceptance, but also looking for either the young, presumably conflicted biological mother I never knew, or a self-assured, stable partner. An anchor. In the former, I imagine I was trying to save my biological mother. In the latter, I was trying to save myself.

My obsession with relationships during college led to one formal engagement – to the daughter of the college dean – and one informal commitment to marry. Because of my insecurities and jealousies, I also ruined two other relationships with women of great intelligence and stability who went on to carve out noble professional careers.

No matter how long a relationship lasted or who engineered the ending, the demise was often gut-wrenching and always confusing. I could never grasp the complexities of a relationship. I could never find a comfortable plateau of belonging. I could never find home.

I did, however, manage to drop the drugs cold turkey. I woke up one chilly, gray morning in Montana and, while lying in bed, noticed the arm of one of my roommates in an adjoining bedroom hanging from the side of his bed. I can't be certain, but I think he may have shot up the night before, and the image of his seemingly lifeless arm was enough to make me realize that, at least where drugs were concerned, I was headed on a path of no return. It helped that a few weeks before that unsettling moment, a college colleague had referred to me as "chemical head." That, too, was an eye-opener.

I found some success in college in the performing arts and made theater my major, likely influenced by seeing Arthur Miller's *The Price* on Broadway—featuring a mesmerizing, stage-commanding performance by character actor Pat Hingle—during a high school field trip. My interest in theater also grew when I landed the lead male role of Alfred Chamberlain, the neurotic photographer in *Little Murders,* after my first college audition. I went on to play other prominent characters, including Nathan Detroit in *Guys and Dolls* and Noah Curry in *The Rainmaker.*

It felt intoxicating to be accepted so readily into the theater fraternity. But the recognition I received from being on stage triggered a vanity that hid the profound hollowness and confusion that roiled inside me. Moreover, acting allowed me to escape into other characters and avoid working on myself. Jumping from part to part was much more comfortable than confronting my internal demons.

I did make some choices that yielded positive results. An adventurous, rugged college friend of mine, Mike McCann, who to this day continues to push the boundaries of geographic and experiential exploration, introduced me to finding oneself through hitchhiking. He was from Long Island and had been hitchhiking back and forth between Montana and his childhood home. His chief piece of advice was this: always hitchhike alone. That way, he said, one doesn't run the risk of dealing with another person's on-the-road issues. It also significantly improves the odds of being picked up.

Three times I hitchhiked the 2,200 miles between Montana and New York. I carried a large green backpack with my lacrosse stick tied to one side. I brought a limited amount of money so I would not be tempted to give up and catch a bus or train. I carried no weapons for protection. The quickest I made the journey was two and a half days; the longest was five days. Not once did I sleep in a motel, instead getting intermittent rest in the back seats of my rides or finding suitable outdoor places along the way for an hour or two of slumber.

I once slept in a roadway culvert south of Caspar, Wyoming, when a snowstorm closed Interstate 25. I dug through the snow to retrieve corn stover—the cobs, leaves, and stalks left after a harvest—from a farmer's field so I could build a nest in the culvert. In the morning, when the interstate reopened, a whiskered codger in a beat-up pickup truck gave me a ride. During another major road-closing snowstorm, I huddled against two delinquent teenagers beneath an Interstate 94 overpass in Sauk Centre, Minnesota. The sleep was sporadic. The shivering was constant. Adversity sometimes made for strange bedfellows.

I encountered all manner of people and situations during my hitchhiking sojourns. Two ex-convicts, traveling in a largely gutted car on Montana's Interstate 90, told me they were heading to a reunion of former prison buddies at a home in Boulder, Colorado, which it turned out was owned by a flighty, wild-eyed, amphetamine-fueled woman. A just-dismissed, pockmarked military man en route to California picked me up at 2 A.M. on Interstate 70 near the Missouri border and asked me to drive across Kansas so he could sleep in the back seat. A blonde woman from Ohio driving a red Mustang convertible along Illinois' Interstate 70 also picked me up; just that morning, she had skipped out on her wedding and wasn't sure where she was headed, other than away. A boyfriend and girlfriend who attended the University of Notre Dame and Saint Mary's College in South Bend, Indiana, were looking for company on their Interstate 80 drive to the east coast. A group of pot-smoking commune members gave me a lift and crept along well below the speed limit in their VW bus on Interstate 80 in Pennsylvania. A businessman driving Interstate 71 outside of Cleveland picked me up because he noticed my lacrosse stick; it turned out his son and I had played lacrosse together in our senior year at Fox Lane High School. Small world.

Surviving those hitchhiking expeditions bolstered my self-confidence. I learned to talk to people in a way that would disarm those who might have malevolent intentions and ease the fears of those who might have found themselves wondering why they had picked up a stranger by the side of the road. I also learned in the lonely, uncertain spaces between rides that I could muster optimism whenever defeat seemed a distinct possibility.

Some of the jobs I held while attending college also added to a reservoir of stability. I learned to cook at a restaurant at the fledgling Big Sky Resort, then owned by famed NBC broadcaster Chet Huntley, who frequently visited the kitchen to order food for out-of-town guests. There was a T-bone named after him on the menu, but he usually ordered hamburgers. I also planted saplings for U.S. Forest Service reclamation projects on remote mountainsides—a monotonous job, but one that afforded views of spectacular expanses. I conditioned cars at a Bozeman dealership one summer and made them look virtually new, never mind that beneath the sparkling exteriors were a host of serious problems. Another summer back in New York, I carried large stones and hand-mixed mortar for two hot-headed Italian masons who spoke little English and communicated with hand gestures and loud voices. They used the phrase "va fungool" at lot when they were mad at me, basically telling me to go screw myself.

My future vocation came not from any of my short-term jobs but from a chance encounter. In my junior year of college, out of curiosity, I poked my head inside the door of the college newspaper, *The Exponent*, and was greeted by the editor, who told me he had an opening for a sports editor. I told him I had virtually no experience as a writer or editor, but when he mentioned the job paid eighty dollars a quarter, I accepted the position. I was quickly hooked by seeing my name in print, learning about a range of subjects by interviewing various people of notable achievements, and being part of an essential institution that served as government watchdog and purveyor of community information.

By this time, I was going by the name Rick Farrant. I still despised my childhood nickname, Ricky, which sounded immature to me, and I disliked Richard because it sounded pretentious. Rick, on the other hand, sounded cool. I now realize that by altering my first name, I also put distance between me and my childhood trauma, helping to create a new me.

Within three weeks of accepting the college newspaper position, filled with confidence I had finally found something I might be good at, I walked into the newsroom of the *The Bozeman Daily Chronicle* and announced to the managing editor that he needed to hire me. He took me on as a general assignment reporter for twenty hours a week at $1.60 an hour.

In hindsight, my early interviews must have been taxing for those on the other side of the table. My lack of knowledge about so many things and my nascent, sloth-like note-taking skills had to have been torture for the people who sat down with me. Fortunately, no one complained.

Sports was something I knew and those interviews usually went well. I had to overcome my awe, though, when I sat down with Montana Bobcat football stars Bill Kollar and Sam McCullum, both of whom went on to have solid careers in the National Football League.

I was, meanwhile, wholly unprepared for an interview with geodesic dome designer Buckminster Fuller. Fuller, a Mensa member of the highest order, was exceedingly courteous, engaged, and spirited as he rambled on about philosophy, theory, and practice in words and complex sentence structures I had never encountered before. When the interview was over, I was left with the sickening feeling that I had understood at best about a tenth of what he had said.

Journalistic missteps notwithstanding, finding an activity that could hold my interest, feed my natural curiosities, and allow me to learn about life through others was a blessing. It would serve me well professionally for many years to come. It would not, however, save me from the dramas that would upend my personal life—dramas that would lead to six marriages and five divorces.

Exploring the environmental and historical splendors of the Rocky Mountain West also played a role in my personal development. I visited Yellowstone National Park south of Bozeman; ghost towns long since abandoned; Pompey's Pillar, a sandstone rock formation that features Native American petroglyphs and an 1806 inscription by explorer William Clark; and Little Bighorn Battlefield National Monument, where the U.S. Army's 7th Calvary led by Lt. Col. George Armstrong Custer was wiped out by a force of Sioux and Cheyenne on Montana's eastern plains.

During the time I was in Montana, the Custer site was named Custer Battlefield National Monument. Appropriately, it was renamed in 1991 to recognize both sides and to avoid celebrating what Native Americans considered part of a genocidal western expansion.

I am disinclined to sugarcoat the atrocities of the European immigrants who, powered by an expansionist government blind to the rights of indigenous people, marched west, stole the lands of the Native Americans, raped their culture by trying to force assimilation, and killed, by some accounts, millions through military aggression and the introduction of disease.

The raw beauty of Montana still pulses inside me, but so too does the knowledge that generations of Native Americans have been forced to eke out marginal existences with limited resources and heritages that are, at best, in tatters. It is far worse, I think, to know one's origins and struggle to fully reconnect than to not know one's origins at all, as was the case with me.

Times, fortunately, may be changing for Native Americans. I was heartened to learn in 2018 that my alma mater would build a center where Native American students could learn about their culture and teach others. I couldn't wait to send a check.

After college, I made half-hearted attempts to learn about my own heritage and locate my birth mother. In my mid-twenties, when my adoptive mother gave me all of the adoption papers she had, the only significant piece of information seemed to be that one name: Richard Alan Shinn. I assumed it was either my real name given me by my birth mother or a fictitious name given me by the adoption agency. I believed the latter, but nevertheless eventually tried to fool the state of New York by representing myself as Richard Alan Shinn and submitting a request for a birth certificate. The state did not fall for my ruse.

Chapter Five

When the internet rolled around, I occasionally searched key words in hopes of finding something about my origins—words like "Richard Alan Shinn Yonkers New York" or "Shinn Yonkers New York." Once, I found an intriguing connection to a Shinn and Yonkers in an obituary for a man who had been born in Yonkers but who had lived for much of his life in New Jersey. His name was Parker Bohn, Sr. His deceased wife's maiden name was Barbara May Shinn and she seemed to have no connection to Yonkers. I quickly dismissed the information.

I also conducted searches for hospitals and high schools that might have been in Yonkers in 1952 and managed to find the names of several high school graduating classes. The name Shinn never surfaced in the graduating classes, at least not in the classes I could find. I also posted my name and adoption information with the ALMA Society and with genealogy.com in case my birth mother was looking for me or if biological relatives knew of her whereabouts. When I received no responses, I assumed she was either dead or disinterested in finding me.

In 1985, at the age of thirty-two and living in Colorado, I wrote the Spence-Chapin Adoption Service seeking non-identifying information about my birth mother and father. The information they sent was tantalizingly incomplete. It included a little about my father and maternal grandparents. It revealed a bit more about my mother: she was a high school graduate, a secretary in her early twenties, five feet ten inches tall, of average build with bright blue eyes, and she enjoyed ice skating and roller skating. They were attributes I would remember from the adoption agency's response, more or less accurately, for the next three decades. I had to rely on memory because I failed to put the agency's letter in a safe place and eventually lost it. At the time, it just wasn't that valuable to me. I couldn't see how any of the information would help me find my birth mother; the descriptions could fit thousands, if not tens of thousands, of people.

Later in life, people sometimes would ask me if I had ever looked for my birth mother. I would tell them I really hadn't, and that if it were truly important to me I would have taken a couple of months off work and done some detective sleuthing in and around Yonkers, including checking microfilm of old newspapers, pouring through city directories and U.S. Census Bureau documents, and conducting interviews with Yonkers residents who were alive in 1952. Surely, I told people, I would have been able to employ my journalistic research skills honed over decades of work at publications such as the *Denver Post*, *Time* magazine, *San Bernardino Sun*, *Danville Commercial-News*, *Hammond Times* and the *Fort Wayne Journal Gazette*.

But I never took that leap. The closest I would come to pulling out all the stops occurred whenever I caught a TV show reuniting a long-lost child with a birth parent. I would cry uncontrollably, chest heaving, happy they had finally found each other and profoundly sad that I might never know who my birth mother was. In those brief moments I knew, all of my excuses aside, how powerful a resolution would be. But I didn't dwell on it. I allowed myself to grieve for as long as the episode lasted, then blew my nose, wiped away the tears with a wad of tissues, and moved on.

What led me to my latest search was a spate of broadcast, digital, and print advertisements promoting DNA analysis kits that promised information about peoples' ethnicities. Also, I was facing the prospect of major surgery to circumvent a life-threatening aortic aneurysm. I had already survived two heart attacks, but the aneurysm, which appeared during a routine forty-nine-dollar test, was so daunting that I felt a need to get my affairs in order—and at the very least learn a little more about my ancestral makeup in case the surgery did not go well. I wasn't looking for my birth mother or other relatives. I wanted to know where I came from in a broader sense.

I chose ancestry.com for no particular reason and, when my results came back on May 9, 2017, I learned I was mostly English and Irish, with a small amount of other ethnicities. I also noticed, much to my surprise, 270 matches for fourth cousins or closer. Most of the relatives were distant and no siblings, half-siblings or parents were listed, but there was a handful of extremely high-probability second or third cousins. In six decades of living, it was the first time that the vague belief I had biological relatives somewhere became concrete reality. I had to catch my breath looking at the online page. I felt inexorably drawn to finally discovering where I came from.

Initially, I randomly chose two second or third cousins, Stasie and Sandra, and sent them messages asking a question that would either eliminate or confirm the value of that name on the adoption papers. Were there, I asked, any Shinns in their ancestry?

Indeed, they replied, there *were* Shinns. Lots of them. And all of a sudden, there it was. A journey I could have never imagined was about to begin.

As a longtime journalist, I try to avoid overstatement, but the realization that I was born with a different name and that I might soon discover my biological roots was earthshaking. I can't think of a better term for it. I had difficulty concentrating on my day job as a communications professional for a workforce development organization. I mindlessly ran stoplights. I went to sleep and awoke mornings ruminating on the possibilities of my origins.

In my sixty-four years, I had learned to effectively compartmentalize—to free myself from anything that might interfere with what was important to me. Work. Finances. Relationships. But the search for my origins became my most vital undertaking, and the initial information-gathering ramped up fast and furious. In a matter of days, other people became passionately engaged in the search; some because they knew and cared about me, some who came to care about me, and some merely drawn by the puzzles of the pursuit.

There were momentary ebbs as we painstakingly gleaned, double-checked and triple-checked new information. But generally, it poured in at a dizzying pace. The most difficult part was the delicate dance of developing trust with newfound biological relatives confronted with jarring information as new to them as it was to me. In some cases, trust wavered; in others, trust was never secured. In still others, lasting bonds were formed.

The research began with three people. A work colleague introduced me to a researcher in Fort Wayne, Indiana, where I've lived for more than two decades.

That researcher, Andra, along with my newfound second cousin Sandra, began looking at family trees based on what was known about Sandra and the other cousin, Stasie. Andra was invaluable in analyzing U.S. Census Bureau information and other online documents and postings.

One thing that surfaced rather quickly was the importance of those two names from the obituary I had dismissed: Barbara May Shinn and Parker Bohn Sr.

Both Stasie and Sandra, it turned out, had one notable connection: Barbara May's father, Harold Page Shinn Sr., who was born in 1895. He lived much of his life in Monmouth County, New Jersey, worked as a railroad telegraph operator, and produced five children from two marriages. A large white board would have come in handy to follow the rest of the trail.

Harold Sr. was first married to Ethel Wilkins, and that union produced two children: Althea Shinn and Harold Page Shinn Jr. Althea (Shinn) Hamelman was born in 1916 and was the grandmother of Stasie, who now lived in Pennsylvania but was born in 1962 in New Jersey. Harold Page Shinn Jr. was born in 1918 and was the father to Sandra, who was born in 1944 in New Jersey with the Shinn name and who now lived in North Carolina.

Harold Page Shinn Sr., Harold Page Shinn Jr. and Althea were all deceased. But one child of Harold Page Shinn Sr.'s second marriage to Florence Lawson survived: Barbara May's sister, Nancy. She was born on May 6, 1930, making her eighty-seven years old at the time my searching began. She still lived in Monmouth County, and was fighting a battle against cancer and a failing heart valve. A third child of Harold Page Sr. and Florence, a son named Howard, was deceased.

Barbara May and Nancy lived in a number of Monmouth County towns growing up, including Manasquan, Farmingdale, Colts Neck and Howell, and both graduated from Freehold High School. Nancy and her husband had two daughters, Carol and Susan, both still living. Barbara May and her husband, Parker Bohn Sr., had three daughters and a son, all still living: Jeanne of Texas, Diane of Tennessee, Lisa of New Jersey, and Eddie of North Carolina.

Recalling that my birth mother had been in her early twenties when I was born, my helpers and I determined that there were only two women in Harold Page Shinn Sr.'s known lineage who would have been approximately that age in

1952—Nancy and Barbara May. Nancy was twenty-two then. Barbara May was twenty. Either, I figured, could be my mother.

What confused me about Barbara May and Nancy is that if one of them was my birth mother, why was I born in Yonkers and not New Jersey? I initially thought that Parker, who was born in Yonkers, might be my father and that Barbara May had possibly stayed with his relatives in Yonkers.

But as my search took root after the ancestry.com results, it dawned on me that unwed mothers back then often traveled to facilities in other locales—that Parker's Yonkers birthplace was likely a coincidence.

I searched online for a home for unwed mothers in Yonkers. I didn't find one, but I did find a now-defunct home for unwed mothers in Tarrytown, New York—St. Faith's House. Various articles said most of the mothers at St. Faith's gave birth at St. John's Riverside Hospital in Yonkers, no more than a dozen miles from the home, and I vaguely recalled my adoptive mother saying I was born in "Riverside Hospital." It now seemed quite possible that Barbara May, or her sister Nancy, could have traveled north from Monmouth County to give birth.

Still another question remained, though: What would prompt someone to go so far, some eighty miles at least, to give birth? I discovered one possible answer when I learned that the services of St. Faith's were well known beyond New York. The home was featured in a March 1938 spread in *LIFE* magazine.

The *LIFE* piece, headlined "Unwed Mothers Care For Their Babies and Forget Their Shame at St. Faith's," described the home as a happy place. Photographs included young mothers holding their newborns; mothers and a white-capped nurse in a room filled with babies at a weekly 'weigh-in day;' and a boisterous celebration of a newborn coming home to St. Faith's.

The text of the article, no matter how well-meaning, illustrated how society once felt about unwed mothers. The article suggested some people might think the young women at the home were sinners underserving of happiness. But the writer described the women as innocent and undeserving of shame – that they demonstrated extraordinary caring as they learned the necessities of motherhood. No mention was made of the fathers' actions that led to the mothers' predicaments.

Almost from the start, I focused on Barbara May in my search. Besides the chance discovery of the Parker Bohn Sr. obituary mentioning Barbara May and her name resurfacing in the ancestry analysis, there were a number of other reasons. I learned through relatives that she was five feet ten and her occupation at the time of her death was secretary/receptionist—the same height and occupation I remembered from the adoption agency letter. Nancy, I would learn, also spent time working as a secretary, but she was only five feet eight.

That information was not proof-positive, but there were two other factors at play. I simply had a general sense, a feeling I could not explain then or now, that Barbara May was my birth mother. I'd heard about inexplicable connections between people. Although those usually apply to people who know each other in life, I had an uncanny sense that Barbara May and I had shared space on this earth before.

The other factor was a photograph of Barbara May I found on the Facebook page of her daughter, Jeanne. Nancy's daughter, Carol, had not yet sent me the photographs of Barbara May, so the black-and-white Facebook photo was the first image I saw of her. Later, relatives would tell me that it was taken in 1974 at one of Barbara May's daughter's weddings when Barbara May was forty-two years old. She was smiling and wore a large corsage, and there was something about her chin, her long jaw line, her eyes and eyebrows, and the slope of her nose at the tip that seemed familiar—and similar to my own features. I looked at that photo more than once and for more than a few minutes each time, zooming in and out looking for one defining characteristic that made a mother-son connection not only plausible, but certain. In the end, I was left with plausible—but a very strong plausible. I longed for Barbara May to be my biological mother.

I also found a photo of Nancy on her daughter Carol's Facebook page that appeared to be current. I found her facial features to be less familiar. Nancy's picture also did not produce the supernatural sense of belonging that Barbara May's picture did. Simply put, I felt an attachment to Barbara May's image. She looked elegant, happy and grounded in the picture. And so out of reach for me.

I knew I had to go to Monmouth County, New Jersey, if only to get a geographical sense of where I might have come from.

Chapter Six

May 27, 2017 was a beautiful, seventy-degree, cotton-cloud day at Brigadier General William C. Doyle Veterans Memorial Cemetery in Wrightstown, New Jersey. Hundreds of cars and motorcycles were parked in rows in a field near an entrance that morning, their occupants there for a Memorial Day weekend observance. The crowd spilled out from white tents in front of a memorial pavilion, two jets shot across patches of blue, and thousands of small, staked graveside American flags lifted and fell and curled in a light breeze that swept across the surrounding hills and dales for as far as the eye could see.

I had taken advantage of the long holiday weekend to drive the roughly seven hundred miles from Fort Wayne to New Jersey, accompanied by a dear workplace colleague of mine, Rafat, who had become greatly interested in my search. My goal: to walk or drive the path of my ancestors now that I knew what part of the country I was from. More specifically, I wanted to visit sites I had learned might be familiar to the two women I had identified as candidates to be my birth mother. That included Barbara May's gravesite.

I made a rather impulsive decision to take the trip, which came just three weeks after receiving the DNA results identifying two of my cousins. But in that short time, I had amassed a growing volume of ancestral and related information. I had, for instance, discovered that Barbara May's husband, Parker Bohn Sr., was a race car driver of some note in New Jersey, and that Barbara May's son, Eddie, and his sons had also become race car drivers. One of Parker Bohn Sr.'s grandsons from an earlier marriage is a member of the Professional Bowlers Association Hall of Fame.

I had also learned that when Barbara May died at work, it was at a New Jersey auto service center owned by the husband of one of her daughters, Lisa. The most chilling aspect of Barbara May's death was that she was struck down by an aortic aneurysm – the same condition for which I would soon undergo surgery. What were the odds, I thought, that a shared malady like that had no significance?

I learned some of this in phone calls I made to two of Barbara May's children: Diane and Jeanne. Andra, the local researcher, and cousin Sandra had found phone numbers for all of Barbara May's children, but only Diane's and Jeanne's were current. I also had phone numbers for Barbara May's sister, Nancy, and her daughters, Carol and Susan. I had reached Carol on Facebook, but I was leery about calling Nancy after Carol messaged me about her mother's medical condition.

I decided arbitrarily that I would call Diane first, and I agonized for three days about how to start the conversation. I could think of no easy way to tell her out of the ether that I, a person she likely never knew existed, might be her half-sibling. I wore myself out trying to conjure up conversation starters and eventually opted to wing it—to let my journalistic experience interviewing and effectively interacting with people take over. It was, appropriately, Mother's Day, and I began the phone call with Diane this way:

"Hello, is this Diane?"

"Yes, who's this?"

"My name is Rick Farrant and this will probably be one of the most peculiar phone calls you will ever receive."

I rolled out my search story—the information I had collected and how I believed that either her mother or Nancy was my birth mother. I did the same with Jeanne in a phone call to her and in correspondences through her Facebook page. The news stunned both Diane and Jeanne, who were understandably dubious about me and my intentions, a bit curious, and in need of more time to absorb what I had shared. Jeanne, in particular, was unnerved that I had found out so much about the Shinn family. Diane wondered why her mother had never told her about me, if in fact her mother was my birth mother.

I explained to Diane and Jeanne that my only interest was to learn the truth about my origins, that I was asking nothing else from them. I would repeat this often to Diane and Jeanne and later to Nancy's daughter, Carol. I never lost sight of the fact that I was not the only one grappling with knowledge that was readjusting long-held understandings, or in my case, guesses, about family histories.

One thing I didn't share with Diane, Jeanne, or Carol was my plan to travel to New Jersey. I believed it would have been too soon for them and would risk exacerbating any fears they might harbor that I was a stalker, a scammer, or otherwise up to no good. I was aware that in today's world, looking over one's shoulder has become the norm, where trust is rarely completely won.

The only relative I told about the New Jersey trip was second cousin Sandra in North Carolina, who had become an essential research collaborator and cheerleader. Whenever a roadblock emerged in the search, Sandra was there through online messages to encourage, prod, and strategize.

I corresponded with Sandra several times during my brief stay in New Jersey, which began at the veterans' cemetery because it was the first point of interest upon our entry into the state. Until we arrived at the cemetery I had forgotten that it was Barbara May's birthday and her twelfth year in heaven, or at least in some ethereal place where she is happy and at peace. Whether from my sometimes confusing, hurtful experiences with harsh judgments associated with organized religion or something else, the traditional concept of heaven—and a being called God, for that matter—had been eclipsed late in life by a belief that the principles of science and other forces we cannot identify provide an energy that dictates our lives and deaths, the miracles and the tribulations. If this combination needs a name, maybe it's God.

Barbara May's birthday wasn't the only thing lost on me that day. I had even ignored the likelihood that the cemetery would be alive with Memorial Day tributes. Such was the singular focus of my mission, one Rafat and I carried out almost to the exclusion of anything else.

In the two days that followed the cemetery visit, and with the irreplaceable help of a GPS, we raced around Burlington and Monmouth counties past old, gnarly trees, weathered barns, historic brick and wood buildings, and straight-line ribbons of railroad track, all the while looking for places that existed when Barbara May and her sister were young. In Freehold, we found the diminutive brick Carnegie Library, circa 1903, where perhaps Barbara May and her sister checked out a book or two; the Freehold Bottle Shoppe with its decades-old script "Freehold" sign; the white Georgian and Gothic Revival St. Peter's Episcopal Church, circa 1771, and still holding services; the white-columned Freehold Fire Department; and the three-story red, ornate building in downtown Freehold, circa 1874, which in 2017 housed a Mexican restaurant on the ground floor.

We visited the old train station, now a bus depot but still bearing a cracking wooden sign announcing "Freehold. Settled – 1715" and still sitting beside tracks—perhaps the same ones my mother took when she headed to Tarrytown, New York to give birth to a baby boy. We also stopped by the auto service center where Barbara May died, and Wall Stadium in Wall, New Jersey, where Barbara May watched Parker and their children race the third-of-a-mile oval to checkered flags.

The auto service center, it turned out, was a modest building with four bays and an adjoining small office. Scores of "Police Benevolent Association Local 50" stickers filled the glass on the front door, and an old Cooper Tires sign on the front counter façade proclaimed: "We make tires for people." Customers could leave their vehicles at the center after hours by dropping keys in an envelope on which they had written their contact information, the kind of service requested, and whether old or new parts were desired.

The service center was closed on Memorial Day weekend and its blinds drawn. But in the small horizontal slivers between the slats, I could discern the layout of the office and the desk area to the left of the counter where Barbara May likely took her last breath—and where at least some pieces of my history were lost forever.

Wall Stadium, meanwhile, was bustling with practice laps before the 7 P.M. Saturday features. The beastly roar of the engines was deafening in the bowl that surrounds the track, and most of those watching in the stands wore ear plugs or protectors. A few old-timers, fans who had been traveling to Wall since the 1950s, didn't remember Barbara May, but they remembered her husband, Parker Bohn Sr., and recalled in gravely voices: "Heckuva driver" or "Oh yeah, he was real good." A dock builder by day, Parker was memorialized in a Wall Stadium trailer that served as the Garden State Vintage Stock Car Club Museum. There, immediately inside the front door, was the hopelessly beat up white door of one of Parker's cars, with his name stenciled in script below the window opening and, beneath that, the trademark "659" in black and red. He had chosen the unique three-digit number because it represented a favorite fan belt of his.

On Ascension Sunday, we visited the white clapboard First United Methodist Church, where Nancy and Carol attend services in a small sanctuary dominated by a façade of towering bronze organ pipes and rich with welcoming parishioners. Before leaving Fort Wayne, I had considered approaching Carol and Nancy after the Ascension Sunday service. But on our way to New Jersey, Carol had sent a message asking me to be patient, that it would take time for her to discuss things gently with her mother.

Carol, whom I recognized from her Facebook photos, attended the service the day Rafat and I were there, sitting no more than six feet in front of us and to the right. Nancy was not there. I spent the entire hour periodically watching Carol, realizing I was for the first time seeing a living biological relative. What I didn't know was whether she was a first cousin or a half-sibling. What I didn't do was approach her after the service, instead honoring her request for patience. The last thing I wanted to do was upend trust and, although the situation was frustrating, I felt confident we would eventually meet.

We also visited the densely populated Greenwood Cemetery in Brielle, where Harold Page Shinn Sr., Barbara May's father, and Florence (Lawson) Shinn, her mother, are buried. Without the benefit of a map, we drove at a crawl along the winding, narrow road weaving between sections of grave markers, looking for headstones that said "Shinn." We never found one.

The same fate almost befell us at the sprawling veterans' cemetery where Barbara May is buried. The cemetery office was closed and, without directions, we calculated it would take us days to carefully walk the grounds. Even then, we figured we might not find her site. But this time luck was on our side. We approached a woman who worked there, explained that we had driven all the way from Indiana, and she agreed to open the office and fetch a map to Barbara May's grave. Section 2, Grave No. 6228, the map read, about a five-minute walk to a field fronting a grove of trees.

What transpired next was wrapped in a bundle of swelling emotions that seemed to take on a life of its own. Blades of grass crept over portions of the bronze plaque memorializing Barbara May and Parker, and so I bent down and pulled them away. It seemed horribly irreverent that the grass was intruding on their grave. A moment later, I found myself sitting, one hand on the plaque, a light breeze sweeping across the vast sea of tiny American flags, a bugler's taps piercing the air from the pavilion ceremony in the distance, and tears, my tears, welling, cascading. It occurred to me then that although I still didn't know if Barbara May was my aunt or my birth mother, it was possible I was for the first time in sixty-four years within feet of my biological origin. And it was in that moment that I allowed myself to fully realize just how important it was to me to know my roots—that I had masked an inherent, burning desire with rational, yet disingenuous, excuses. I had been protecting myself against the possibility that I would never know.

Sitting next to the grave stripped me of my defenses, and I began the conversation I'd waited decades to have. It wasn't perfect, because there was so much I still didn't know. Nearly every sentiment, more mouthed than uttered aloud, was preceded by, "If you're my mother Barbara May…." or "I don't know for sure if you're my mother, but if you are…" I began by wishing her a happy birthday—and that came with no condition attached. It was, after all, Barbara May's birthday and I was, in fact, related to her in some way. Then I conditionally thanked Barbara May for giving me life—if in fact she had done that—and perhaps a better life than she could have provided as a single mother. I empathized with her presumed situation in 1952 and I told her I hoped that, all things considered, she'd had a happy life. Then I thanked her again. And again. I told her that, all things considered, my life had been a good one. In the next breath, I abandoned all caution: "I turned out okay, Mom," I said. "I think you would have been proud of me."

What I didn't expect amidst my tears of long-awaited discovery was the powerful sadness of knowing I likely would never be able to see my mother again. I would never be able to touch her or feel her touch me, or look in her eyes, or hear her voice.

I also didn't expect a flicker of anger. The Shinn family seemed to have closely guarded the secret of my existence and that, along with the state of New York's laws, made it difficult for a child to at least learn about his origins from afar and at most thank his mother in person for a great gift bestowed. Sitting on the grass that day in the bucolic cemetery surrounded by horse farms, it didn't comfort me to rationalize, as I had done so many times, that out-of-wedlock pregnancies in the middle of the twentieth century were embarrassing history not to be discussed by the generations that followed. In that short-lived anger, and for the first time in my life, I grew selfish about my right to know about me.

When the anger passed and the tears subsided, I no longer allowed the thought that Barbara May might not be my birth mother. I was lost in the belief that she was, and I didn't want to leave her again, not that I ever wanted to or had a choice in the first place. I wanted to lie in the grass beside her. I wanted to wipe away her tears now long since gone. I wanted to hug her and whisper that everything with us was okay. I wanted to fall asleep, maybe forever, in an eternal embrace of souls connected not just by genetics, but by the inherent bonds of a mother's love for her son and a son's love for his mother. I wanted to do what I couldn't do six decades earlier: protect her.

Chapter Seven

Fresh from the New Jersey trip, I persuaded Jeanne, one of Barbara May's daughters, to submit a DNA sample to ancestry.com in the hopes the results would remove any doubt about who my birth mother was. I also sent a letter to the adoption agency asking them to resend the non-identifying information I had lost thirty-two years earlier, which I knew described not only my mother but also my maternal grandmother and grandfather and included a little about my father. I just couldn't remember all of the details.

A week later, the childhood and teenage photos of Barbara May arrived from Carol, followed by photos of Barbara May later in life, her husband, her grandchildren, her son Eddie, and her older sister Nancy and younger brother Howard. A week after that, Carol sent the eulogy Nancy read at Barbara May's funeral in 2005.

I was grateful for the frenetic pace of the developments, feeling a great urgency to know the truth about my birth mother before my aortic aneurysm surgery a mere two months away. Although optimistic about the operation, my surgeon said the location of the aneurysm made it an unusually challenging procedure and, with any surgery, complications were possible. If I was going to die, I wanted to check out with the answers to my origins.

Nancy's eulogy filled in a few holes, but I wanted more, needed more. In addition to describing Barbara May's love of animals, the eulogy highlighted her nurturing nature with children and her lifelong maternal instincts:

I've known Barbara her entire life—I am her sister. Our father was a telegrapher for the Pennsylvania Railroad. Our mother was a nurse, and we grew up in a series of towns along the Jersey shore with our parents and little brother, Howard. Things have changed a lot since we grew up. Back in those days, there was no TV or video games and certainly no computers, so we had to make our own fun.

We used to play house in the woods behind our home, when the only thing you had to be afraid of while in the woods was the Jersey Devil.

When we lived in Farmingdale during World War II, there was a junkyard next door. We'd spend hours and hours playing in overturned cars pretending they were tanks.

Late one afternoon, when we were about five and seven years old, I remember taking Barbara by the hand, heading through our back yard in Collingswood Park, in search of the setting sun. In a very short time, the sunset ended and so did our adventure.

Through our childhood, we shared a bedroom and lots of sibling rivalry. I think Barbara's first words to me were, 'Don't touch me.' So each night before we went to sleep, I'd lean over to her and whisper in her ear, 'Don't touch me.' It was somewhat hard to ignore each other when we also shared a very tiny bed in that very tiny room.

When our little brother, Howard, came along, Barbara was thrilled. She was especially close to him and always wanted to take care of him. Her mothering instincts kicked in very early in her life.

Barbara's love for animals started when she was a small child. Often our mother would say, "I wonder what kind of sick or hurt animal Barbara will bring home today" to love, nurture and nurse back to health. Our home hosted an endless parade of dogs, cats, birds, chicks, pigs, and ducks.

Her love of animals was passed down to her children. For her daughter, Jeanne, this love started out as a hobby with the 4H and the horses and turned into a career of breeding cats.

For Lisa, it was just last week that she found a baby doe all alone in the woods behind her house and comforted it while searching for its mother.

My sister's nurturing ways shone through when Eddie was admitted to the hospital as a young boy. In those days, parents weren't allowed to stay overnight with their children and I can remember when we walked out of the hospital together, Barbara heard a cry and just knew it was Eddie. It broke her heart to leave him behind. Barbara was like that with all of her children.

Diane lived next door to her childhood home in the early years of her marriage and Barbara loved having her first two grandchildren so nearby. Diane's talent for numbers and accounting knowledge must have rubbed off on her mother when more than fifteen years ago she was thrown into doing the secretarial/receptionist work at (the service center) after Lisa broke her pelvis. What was originally a temporary job while Lisa was recovering became a full-time permanent position until the day she died at her desk, surrounded by her daughter, Lisa, son-in-law and grandson. They were by her side providing the love, care, and comfort that Lisa was taught at an early age.

She loved her children each in their own unique way. She adored her grandchildren too and was especially proud that she had eight of them—all boys. She was thrilled that the next generation started with a great granddaughter, the first girl in the family in almost forty-five years.

One of her other loves was racing and that's where she met her husband, Parker, and the rest is history as she watched her husband, son, sons-in-law, and her grandson race. Even her daughters raced in the Powder Puff Derbies. She spent many hours in the grandstands with Betty, who has been a very dear lifelong friend. You knew never to invite Barbara to anything on a Saturday night because that was her night at the races.

As we grew older, our sibling rivalry of 'don't touch me' became a unique friendship. Although we didn't see each other as

> often as we would have liked, we always knew that we were just a phone call away.
>
> For many years, Barbara watched her family win races. Now she has her own checkered flag. May she rest in peace.

The references to car racing and railroading were utterly foreign to me and raised the specter that had my birth mother kept me, the course of my personal and professional life would have been different. We often gravitate to things that are familiar to us, and in Monmouth County car racing and to a greater extent horse racing were and continue to be major sources of entertainment. Railroads, meanwhile, were once king in Monmouth County. Many residents worked for the railroads, which took Monmouth County commuters to New York City and tourists to Monmouth County for oceanfront and inland activities along the Jersey Shore.

Other relatives confirmed Barbara May's love for children, which I found heartwarming and indicated that, if Barbara May was my birth mother, her decision to give me up for adoption was not just an act of practical necessity, which the legal papers suggested, but was also an act of love. It was more than possible that my birth mother did, in fact, hold me, look into my eyes, and give agonizing consideration to the prospect of keeping and raising me on her own.

It also became clear after reading the eulogy that Barbara May would not have used the crude legal word "abandon" to describe putting a child up for adoption, although that may have been how she would've felt about such a decision. She probably would have felt guilt about sending a child away—a guilt she would have wrestled with in the succeeding years and perhaps assuaged with a name: Richard.

That name is a recurring feature of relatives of the Bohn and Shinn families. Barbara May's husband's father had the middle name Richard. It's also the middle name she gave her son Eddie. I may never know if Eddie's middle name is an homage to Barbara May's father-in-law or in remembrance of me. Nevertheless, it would be reasonable to consider there's a chance that the memory of me was kept alive, in a small measure, through a middle name.

My adoptive parents, meanwhile, said they named me Richard, no middle initial, in honor of one of my adoptive father's brothers, who was killed in a military accident. It's also possible they recognized that Richard was a name I was accustomed to for the first five months of my life before I was placed in their home. Keeping the first name would have made the transition for me easier.

The possible name connection was one of two significant developments that occurred while I waited for Jeanne's DNA test results and the letter from the adoption agency. The other was that Carol gradually began talking to her mother about me. Nancy maintained more than once that she was not my mother. Then one day she shared a stunning recollection: She vaguely recalled a train trip that she, Barbara May, and aunt Anastasia took to Tarrytown, New York, so Barbara May could give birth to a baby. Nancy remembered little else, except that she assumed the baby's father was Parker, who was married at the time but who knew Barbara May long before he obtained a divorce and married her. Nancy believed that it was Anastasia who arranged the trip to New York.

I pressed Carol over several weeks to see if her mother could remember more. But Nancy's memories remained cloudy, obscured by time and a commitment to protect Barbara May's privacy ("It's her story to tell"). Also, as adults, the two sisters were never quite close enough to share the detailed events of each other's lives.

The journalist in me finds it difficult to believe that Nancy would not have asked questions about the origins of the baby. Perhaps, though, the stigma of an out-of-wedlock birth in 1952 made it too difficult to pry.

Two of Barbara May's children, Jeanne and Diane, initially expressed doubt that Nancy's recollection was correct. They had spent a lifetime believing their relationship with their mother was close enough that she would have told them about a secret pregnancy. Nancy's account was also in question, they suggested, because due to the sibling rivalry between Barbara May and Nancy, they believed it possible one might assign the pregnancy to the other.

Indeed, Barbara May and Nancy couldn't have been more different. Nancy was, and still is, the cautious one, protective of her thoughts and not eager to stray from the straight and narrow. Nancy, in an eventual interview, described Barbara May as a "tester"—someone prone to adventure, bending the rules, defying authority, and being outspoken at time when young women were not supposed to do that. "Barbara," Nancy said, "kind of did her own thing in her own way."

But despite the personality differences, the sisters both managed to nurture long marriages—Barbara May for fifty years and Nancy for forty-one. It's all the more noteworthy that they achieved this in the aftermath of such tumultuous childhoods.

I could have used some lessons from them, because transitioning to a well-rounded adult with a confident perspective about relationships would take the better part of my life. My lack of suitable models for marriage and fatherhood, a yearning for acceptance wherever it might be, and the sense that I never really belonged anywhere led to the six marriages—five of which began well, but descended into chaos and finally obliteration.

I was also beset by recurring bouts of diagnosed depression and panic attacks that at times made it impossible for me to find sound emotional footing. Anyone who has been through clinical depression knows the feeling of utter emptiness. Anyone who has been through the incessant cycle of panic attacks knows the breathless, heart-pounding feeling of a mind and body out of control. Both disorders robbed me of the ability to think clearly or act rationally, especially in marriage, which in its healthiest state requires a consistent, balanced perspective.

The stress-induced panic attacks first surfaced during my second marriage. Once I was convinced I didn't have a brain tumor or some other kind of life-threatening malady, I spent years trying to curb the attacks; first with prescription drugs, then breathing exercises, and finally attentive self-monitoring that enabled me to discern when I was susceptible to the attacks. Eventually, I learned to temper my anxiety before it bubbled up into a physiological boil.

My third marriage in particular, which produced two of my three sons, was significantly damaged by my mental health struggles. In my early forties, I spent two weeks in a behavioral health facility in West Lafayette, Indiana, being treated for depression. I had no appetite, no hope, and no clear vision of how to rise above the suffocating bleakness. Virtually every night during my stay there, I lay on my stomach in bed gripping the side rails, worried about what I might do to myself or what the world might do to me. During the day, I took my medications and attended all of the group sessions, many of which were punctuated by patients' life stories that sounded much more calamitous than mine. I sensed that their struggles resulted from things that were done to them, therefore they deserved care. I believed that I was there largely because of things I had done to myself and felt unworthy of empathy. I had worked too hard in my job, wrongly perceived that I was underappreciated at home, and had strayed from my marriage. Guilt about my personal failures consumed me and triggered my mental instability. In short, I snapped and entered a space of disembodiment with no firm connection to reality.

I remember most the day all the patients boarded a bus for a trip to a bowling alley, apparently a regular activity. On the way there, I looked down from my seat and noticed then-Purdue University Basketball Coach Gene Keady driving his car alongside the bus. He was in the real world. I wasn't. When we got to the bowling alley, the distance between the real world and us was even more apparent. There we were—the "crazies" in one set of lanes and the "normals" in another. I'm certain the proprietors knew who we were and I suspect some of the other patrons did too. I can only imagine the whispers.

I didn't think about it at the time, but I now realize my wife must have been terrified at the prospect of losing her husband to insanity and leaving her with two small children to raise alone. I'm certain she couldn't fully understand the darkness that enveloped me, although she tried. She bravely hung in there through the height of the crisis, but between that and my history of erratic behavior, the marriage didn't survive. My wife took the kids, moved away, and remarried. I blamed her then for the breakup, unable to admit my own shortcomings to her or anyone else. I don't blame her now.

In all, my marriages produced three sons and an adopted daughter, recurring heartaches, no lasting friendships with any of my ex's, and estrangement from my sons. To this day, I am haunted by the fact that, despite my fervent hope that I could provide the kind of warm, safe, and loving environment for my sons that I lacked growing up, I failed. I think they hold me responsible for the divorces from their mothers, and one son from my third marriage told me that he did not want to rekindle our relationship because it would bring back the pain of the family separation. I have apologized to him several times over the years to no avail.

It is too agonizing for me at this point to hope that my sons will reenter my life in more than a passing way. One son from my first marriage wants no contact whatsoever. He and his wife have children that I will likely never meet. The two sons from my third marriage have sometimes acknowledged the greetings I send to them on their birthdays and holidays, but they never reciprocate. The damage, I guess, is done.

People say that both people in a tattered marriage are responsible for the breakup. And while there is some truth to that, I am comfortable accepting the bulk of the responsibility in most cases. For much of my life, I did not know who I was, and living with me was not easy. I was wholly fearful of abandonment and rejection, could not seem to sustain any measure of consistent affection for my wives, and I was an obstinate right-fighter. If I thought for a moment my significant other was ready to bolt, I prepared to run first.

The only marriages where I didn't think about exiting first was my first, which ended in a bitter divorce, and my sixth, which ended in a tortuous death. And it's quite possible that the drama of that first marriage, which I went into with naïve optimism and eyes wide shut, helped set the stage for decades of turbulent relationships.

Her name was Marilyn, a willowy, divorced mother of one with a lively smile and personality, and she was the girlfriend of a friend of mine at Montana State. I became so smitten with her that I missed the first warning signs: her son was living with her ex-husband in Marilyn's native Ohio, and she was half a country away more or less simply having fun. Moreover, Marilyn did not hesitate in taking an interest in me at the expense of her boyfriend. One of my biggest regrets is accepting her overtures, not only because of the disastrous outcome of our union, but also because I had violated the trust of a friend.

I paid a large price. Marilyn's vivaciousness, once so engaging and delightful, turned sour and she became physically and emotionally abusive almost the minute after we married in Bozeman, Montana on April 9, 1975. Her abuse continued after we moved to Helena, Montana, where, at the age of twenty-two, I had taken a communications job with the commissioner of higher education and where our son was born. Her demeanor didn't get any better when we later moved to the Midwest so she could be closer to family.

She taunted me to hit her; she locked me out of the house at all hours of the night and morning; and she once held me at knifepoint in our kitchen when she didn't want me to go to work. I was perpetually struggling to save our marriage, myself, and our son, whom Marilyn nearly scalded when she flung a pot of boiling water at me as I held him.

One day, I snapped. We were living in a trailer in Bozeman and had started arguing. She was inches from my face and had a crazy smile that seemed to intimate she was enjoying the experience.

"Go on, hit me," she said.

"I will not hit you," I said.

"Well, then you're a wimp."

"I'm a wimp because I won't hit you? That makes no sense, Marilyn."

"You're a wimp!"

I walked away from her and went to a closet to fetch some rags so I could diffuse the situation by doing some household cleaning. But as I knelt down to get the rags, she grabbed my hair and yanked it. Without thinking, I rose and swung with an open hand, hitting her hard on her left cheek. I was so horrified at what I had done that I raced from our mobile home, got in my car, and drove to the sheriff's office to turn myself in. I knew Gallatin County Sheriff John Onstad well because I had covered a number of criminal cases he had been involved with, including the much-publicized arrest of a serial killer. After I left Montana, he achieved even greater national notoriety for criticizing the actions of Madison County Montana Sheriff Johnny France, accusing France of grandstanding for going it alone in apprehending the abductors of Montana State University biathlete Kari Swenson. The case is memorialized in the book "Incident at Big Sky."

On the day I hit Marilyn, I found Onstad in his office reclining in his chair with his boots up on his desk. He was the epitome of a country lawman, and I mean that in the nicest way possible. He was tough and resistant to excuses, but he was also caring and cunningly smart when it came to assessing the character of a person.

"I've done something terrible, John," I said, trembling. "I hit my wife. You need to arrest me."

He didn't budge. He just laughed.

"No, I'm serious, John. You need to arrest me."

He lowered his boots from the desk, sat up and leaned forward, and listened as I told him what had happened.

"Suppose," he said, "I come out to your place? Talk to her for a bit and see if we can get things settled down?"

And that's exactly what he did. He spoke to Marilyn in fatherly tones and it helped in the moment. But his words of wisdom had no long-term effect on Marilyn's behavior. Most of the time, she was just downright mean.

I had dreamed of a white-picket-fence existence, but ended up mired in domestic chaos. Ultimately, I came home one day to our duplex in Hammond, Indiana, to find Marilyn packing up our one-year-old son and the contents of the house for a new life in Columbus, Ohio, without me. She left behind a small black-and-white TV on the living room floor, and I found what was left of my clothes in a closet. She had taken a pair of scissors or a knife and cut them to smithereens. Not until much later did I realize I had been a victim of domestic violence and abuse.

Perhaps I tolerated Marilyn's behavior, in part, because I was abused by my father and lacked self-esteem. Perhaps it was because I had witnessed my mother tolerating my father's abuse. But an even greater reason may be that, at the time, I thought of domestic abuse as something perpetrated on women, not men. I'd never heard about women abusing men. I had also felt it was my responsibility to endure until I found a solution, much the way I had endured my father's abuse while I worked to figure out how to deal with his physical and verbal assaults. If I could just be a better person, I had thought, maybe the abuse would stop.

In any event, Marilyn filed for divorce shortly after leaving and quickly gained custody of our son. I had lacked the financial resources to fight for him.

I was heartbroken at the loss. More than that, I was worried about my son's safety with a clearly unstable woman, and so I made plans to drive to Columbus to retrieve him, to kidnap him.

On the first try, I walked into his Columbus daycare, passed the unattended front desk, and found my son sleeping in a room with other toddlers. Before I could snatch him, an employee walked in, asked me who I was, and said she was going to call Marilyn to see if it was okay if I took the child for a visit. The gig was up and I left.

Several months later and still determined, I visited Marilyn and my son at a large apartment complex where they were living with Marilyn's mother and her mother's boyfriend. I distracted Marilyn with casual conversation on the back porch as my son bounced in a playpen nearby. Heart pounding, I silently counted to ten, reached into the playpen, grabbed my son, and began running toward my car. A friend, who later became my second wife, had come with me and was in the driver's seat with the engine running, ready for a getaway. But the boyfriend of Marilyn's mother began chasing me and caught up just as I handed the front half of my son to my friend through the open driver's side window. The boyfriend took hold of my son's legs, my friend grasped my son tighter, my son began crying, and I watched several seconds of a fierce tug-of-war. It was heart-wrenching.

"Let him go," I finally said.

My friend looked at me to make sure that's what I wanted.

I nodded. "Let him go."

It was over.

When my son was two and a half, Marilyn called me, said she could no longer take care of him, and I got him back—legally. Marilyn then disappeared, and for the next five years, my son lived with me and my second and third wives. Every time he asked about his mother, I assured him, without knowing if it was true, that she had some personal matters to attend to and that she would be back. I could never tell him when that would be, but I never spoke badly about his mother.

Marilyn resurfaced in Florida when my son was seven and she asked to see him. I hesitated, but she sounded well and I thought seeing his mother would help my son with his feelings of abandonment. I sent him to Florida by plane for what was supposed to be a one-week visit. But when the week was up, Marilyn notified me she would not be returning him, daring me to contest custody in court. I didn't. I had neither the emotional energy nor the money to challenge her from another state, and I also didn't want to subject our son to continued upheaval. I would not see him again until he was an adult.

In the intervening years, I dutifully paid the court-ordered child support that Marilyn had sought. I initially challenged her filing before an Indiana magistrate, noting that I had not sought child support from Marilyn during the years she was MIA. I was more focused, I told the magistrate, on assuming and carrying out my parental responsibility. The magistrate told me I was a fool, reinforcing my feelings of inadequacy.

The Marilyn saga was a long nightmare. The turmoil of our brief marriage and the constant uncertainty about our son's living arrangements left him with emotional scars that would color his own struggle for identity. In my case, I was driven deeper into my low self-esteem and doubt about my worth. For nearly forty years, I hated Marilyn for what she had done to our marriage and to our son.

But I was reminded by Nancy's eulogy for Barbara May that in death, no matter the rifts between two people, a heightened civility, perhaps even a repaired love, emerges. That happened with Marilyn and me.

In early 2013, Marilyn contacted me from her home in Florida to let me know she had terminal cancer. She also had a request: that I write a letter to our son for her that both apologized for the parenting mistakes we had made and to ask him to visit her before she died. By that time, our son had developed a fierce animosity toward both of us and had not spoken to me in more than six years.

I agreed to write the letter for Marilyn, and that led to phone calls and emails between us in which she sought reassurance that there was a place in heaven for her despite her transgressions. She also used our correspondences to work through her fears about death and to apologize to me more than once about her abusive, combative behavior during our marriage. At times, she deflected her concerns with humor. At others, she was sweet, sincere and wistful.

In February 2013, she wrote this email:

> Er, because I respect your opinion. No, I'm not suicidal. I had a PET scan last week. Appears the cancer has spread to the other kidney, other side of the lung, and possibly the brain.
>
> Since I saw my sister Melinda die such a horrific death, even then, five years ago, I vowed I'd never go that way (hospice).
>
> I have been praying on this for months, doing research, researching the Bible, all I can do to make a good decision for a good death—not like my sister, who had tissue coming from her vagina, rotted bowels, lupus celebritas (in her brain). She was an RN for hospice and had planned on euthanasia, but the good old Catholic Church with its fire and brimstone kicked in and she was afraid of going to hell (not in the Bible). So she died a death that no one could imagine.
>
> I want to be with my loved ones and die without pain. Since I don't have control over anything else in my life, I must firmly hold on to how I wish to die. I am not afraid anymore (which was the biggest obstacle), and I'm at peace. No, I have no plan at the moment.
>
> Just want your opinion. What would you do?"

I never gave her a definitive answer, but we went through all the possibilities over the phone. Just talking about it with someone seemed to help her. Four months later, and after I'd written the letter for her to send to our son, I received this email letting me know our son had called her and apparently left a voice mail:

> Thank you.
> I don't know why he called and I hope it wasn't for money, but I can pretend (at least once) it was to be nice.
> I'd rather live with that.
> I really did the best job I could. The kids always came first. Yes, I made many mistakes but they were related to me, not my kids. I wish I could do it over again.

Our son eventually did visit Marilyn, and that buoyed her spirits. In the weeks after his visit, she was grateful for my support and more resigned to her fate. At one point, she wrote, "Let's see. Four active cancers—nah—not going to make it. Just have to wait and see which one hits first and hardest. I'm taking bets (Hedge: the bone cancer—dead in three weeks)."

I asked her in an email to make sure I would be notified when she died:

> As morbid as this may sound, please tell someone to call me—or email me—when your time comes. In the privacy of my own place of reflection, I want to mark yours as a life that mattered and pray for your ascension to a haven where pain has no home. In the meantime, Marilyn, live. As deeply as you can.

I received my last email from her on Christmas Day 2013:

> Merry Christmas.
> Rick: thank you. For lots of things—being my very good friend who understands me (after all these years) and truly cares. This year will be good to you.

She died a month later—on Jan. 23, 2014. She was sixty-one. I received the notice of her death in a group email from one of her daughters, whom I had never met.

The post-marriage relationship I developed with my first wife, and the resolution of our fractured beginnings, was one of the more healing moments in my life. Mixed in with the melancholy was the realization that decades of festering anger and pain had vanished.

Chapter Eight

Before reconciling with Marilyn, my work sustained me through my sequence of marriages, all of them to some degree tumultuous. Journalism can be a stressful, adrenaline-charged business that wears people out, especially those seeking a more favorable work-life balance. But my work became my sanctuary and as time went on, I gained a level of proficiency and confidence in my professional life that I couldn't find in my personal life. Like theater, journalism allowed me to escape into the lives of others as an observer. It felt safe and relatively predictable.

Journalism also served as a looking glass through which I could continue shaping my own identity and beliefs. The newspaper and magazine interviews I conducted with thousands of people over the years offered unique insights into the human experience—the successes and failures, the strengths and frailties, the opportunities seized or missed, and the lessons learned. In large part, I came away with what I believe is this truth: we may all, as the cliché goes, put our pants on the same way and that makes us very much alike, but what sets people of accomplishment apart is that they persevere. I was also struck by the genuine goodness of most people once they set aside their public personas, and I always looked for the real person during my interviews. I did not tolerate superficiality well, nor was I ever impressed with small talk.

The interviews that stood out most were remarkable not by the level of a person's accomplishment or celebrity, but by their raw humility, humanity, and in many cases, intelligence. The firing-on-all-cylinders intellects of comedian George

Carlin and TV broadcasters Mike Wallace and Bill Moyers inspired me; they possessed a profound ability to convey complex ideas with resonant clarity. The genuine warmth of actress Debbie Reynolds and gospel singer Bill Gaither—as well as most of the dozens of country music stars I interviewed—gave me great confidence that the human race, no matter its foibles, had enough good people to survive. "Garfield" creator Jim Davis, who graciously gave me an autographed illustration, singer David Crosby, who played and then signed my guitar, and singer John Mellencamp, who took time to give me advice about recovering from a heart attack, demonstrated that generosity is an essential food for a person's soul.

I was equally struck by the private peculiarities, occasional introversions and everyman insecurities of people in the public spotlight. Among them was Carlin, who in the silent darkness backstage before a performance appeared not as the silver-tongued, full-on critic of social missteps, but as a diminutive, withdrawn man incapable of rhetorical craft. Another one was Ian Anderson of Jethro Tull, who in private dressed more like a mild-mannered high school music teacher than the vibrant pied piper of rock n' roll and who, long before the coronavirus pandemic emerged, insisted on greeting people by touching elbows instead of shaking hands.

Some, like all of us, had doubts about their worth and needed honest appraisals, not idolatry. Scott Thompson (alias Carrot Top) sincerely and with a concerned look asked if I thought his performance one night was good. Country singer Merle Haggard periodically glanced to the wings offstage seeking approval from me and several friends during and after songs. And dc Talk singer Michael Tait surveyed a large, gathering concert crowd one night and worried about whether attendees would be receptive.

I even learned from the unsavoriness of some celebrities that accomplishment without class is no accomplishment at all. There was the retired baseball star with a checkered past who described his sexual predatory escapades by saying, "A stiff dick ain't got no conscience." Or the megastar singer who aggressively picked his nose throughout an entire interview and argued with his wife, who was busying herself nearby.

There were also those of lesser fame whose courage, shared intimately with me during my journalistic work, deeply influenced my ever-developing perspectives on life and the human condition. Among them were George Smith, who was a Congress of Racial Equality (CORE) leader in Meridian, Mississippi, when three fellow activists were murdered in 1964, and Dave Roberts, a Denver cop who survived being shot in the face at point-blank range while making an arrest in 1985. The personalities of those two men couldn't have been more different, but they shared a steadfast commitment to distinguishing between right and wrong in the midst of life-threatening situations.

Some of the people I interviewed flirted with celebrity before returning to a more pedestrian life. Most memorable was Harley Parnell Hisner, a native of tiny Maples, Indiana, and that state's version of Archie "Moonlight" Graham. Hisner learned to pitch by throwing a baseball at the side of a barn, toiled in the minor leagues for several years, and in 1951 made his major league debut with the Boston Red Sox in game against the New York Yankees. He gave up three runs and seven hits in six innings, striking out Mickey Mantle twice. He never made it to the show again, eventually returning home to work, raise a family, and in his advancing years delighting in talking baseball with the local paperboy. He lived a middle class life with no regrets.

Then there were the people lurking in the underbelly of society who had little or no redeeming value, like the consummate con man in Calumet City, Illinois, who was once featured in a column by Chicago journalist Mike Royko. He invited me and a colleague to a motel room guarded by a menacing-looking man with gun, said he was about to flee to the west coast, and asked us to go with him. We didn't take him up on his offer, but the lesson learned was that we are all only one circumstance away from evil, no matter what our station is in life. Two internationally known performers, a comedian and a singer/actress, were among the victims of one of the man's cons.

When it came to writing, I learned from authors of various genres, including James Patterson, Richard Paul Evans and Nora Roberts. There wasn't a single interview I did with an author when I didn't take the opportunity to mine their knowledge about the craft of storytelling—and sometimes in the process get into spirited debates about plot lines and story organization.

The truth is, though, I didn't have to go far to explore the art of writing and editing. The hundreds of journalists I either edited or wrote alongside provided a learning lab of the highest order, and nowhere was that more invigorating than the almost seven years I spent at the Pulitzer Prize-winning *Denver Post* as an assistant city editor and for a short time Sunday editor. Jim Carrier and John A. Farrell—who became noted authors—and Patrick O'Driscoll and Marjie Lundstrom introduced me to the nuances of good writing and put up with my self-perceived ineptitude; Marilyn Robinson, one of the most adept crime reporters I've ever known, showed that through savvy source development, the beat could be handled without venturing outside the newsroom; and Todd Engdahl, Gay Cook, Jere Wales, and Cynthia Pasquale, all incredibly meticulous, demonstrated the value of commitment to accuracy.

These and many other journalists I worked with throughout my career helped shape me as a person and as an award-winning professional, including those I supervised early in their careers, before their stars rose to notable heights. People like Mark Potok, who became a senior fellow at the Southern Poverty Law Center; Doug Haddix, who became the executive director of Investigative Reporters and Editors; Carole Leigh Hutton, who became a top Knight Ridder executive, and Yamil Berard, who continues her fine journalistic work at the Atlanta Journal-Constitution.

Being accepted by all of these people, though sometimes grudgingly, gave me a measure of belonging. More than that, every day that they allowed me the privilege of having a place in their sharp-minded world gave me a modicum of hope that I wasn't as dimwitted as I thought.

We debated content, leads and endings, pace and flow, word choices and transitions, and appropriate lengths. Although the conversations occasionally got testy, the wrangling was rarely about ego. The focus was almost always about improving the storytelling.

There were also the colorful characters in the journalistic fraternity, mostly old-timers who came up through the ranks when journalists wrote their stories on old typewriters and glued the pages together in long strings of paper; when some editors wore green visors and tucked pencils behind their ears; and when it was common for journalists to chain smoke on deadline and sneak a quick nip from flasks hidden in their desks. Some of their imperfections gave me comfort that I was not the only person in the world who could succeed without fitting a "normal" mold.

The Denver Post's "Cap'n" Billy Myers, one of the finest all-around journalists west of Mississippi, was among the characters to cross my path. The crew-cutted

Midwest native was a tobacco-chewing, plain-talking reporter who wore white socks and baby blue jumpsuits with pocket protectors. He was forever leaning over the side of his desk at *The Denver Post* to spit his chew into a waste basket filled with shredded paper and bemoaning his belief that his work was underappreciated. "Of course," he would grouse, "they give all the good stories to the young superstars." Those young superstars, had they been paying attention, would have strived to emulate his folksy interview style, which could disarm even the most cautious person.

Another character was Clint Wilkinson, a cantankerous, hard-driving editor at the *Hammond Times* in Indiana who, although he was small in stature, could strike fear in anyone with his sharp criticisms and steely glint. One day, on deadline, his tie became hopelessly stuck in the warped drawer of his metal desk. He reached for a pair of scissors, snipped the tie at its midpoint, and walked around for the rest of the day with half a tie, daring with a glare anyone to make a remark. No one did.

In idle moments of reflection, memories of all of these people run through me and serve as a reminder that we are more the tapestry of our experiences than the stamp of our origins.

Chapter Nine

In the days leading up to my July 19, 2017 surgery to bypass the aortic aneurysm with an erector set of stents, two things happened that virtually assured Barbara May was my mother.

Jeanne's ancestry.com results came back and her centimorgan count, a simple, relatively reliable genetic measurement for determining biological relationships, was 1,938. That was at the high end of a range (1,450-2,050) that indicated she was a grandparent, aunt, uncle or half-sibling to me. Her age and gender ruled out grandparent, aunt, and uncle, leaving half-sibling as the only conclusion. It also strongly suggested that Barbara May was my mother and Parker Bohn Sr. was not my father.

Jeanne remained doubtful about my connection to Barbara May, largely because she still thought Carol's mother, Nancy, might be my mother, and because half-siblings were at the time generally referred to in ancestry.com by the catch-all category of first cousins. It didn't help that the website also referred to true first cousins the same way.

But I had also convinced Carol to submit her DNA. That way, we could compare her centimorgan count in relation to me with Jeanne's. If Carol's count came up in the true first cousin range (680-1,150), we would be a step closer to definitively defining Barbara May and me as mother and son.

By this time, I had few doubts. The Spence-Chapin adoption agency resent the non-identifying information they had first mailed me in 1985. It arrived two days before my surgery and included too many verifying circumstances and characteristics to be rendered mere coincidence:

Dear Mr. Farrant,

I am writing to share with you the background information you requested in your letter. As you may know, we are not able to give you identifying information but would be pleased to give you descriptive material about your parents from our records.

Your birth mother was a single Caucasian Protestant woman in her early 20's at the time of your birth. She was of English and German descent, was 5'10" tall, of average build, with bright blue eyes, fair complexion and wavy dark hair. She was a high school graduate who was working at the time as a secretary. She enjoyed sports, ice-skating and roller-skating in particular, and liked to cook and to knit. She appears to have been in good health, had had some of the usual childhood diseases and an appendectomy at the age of 11.

Her mother, your maternal grandmother, was a very handsome woman of English descent, who was quite musical. She had had rheumatic fever as a child and her death in her thirties was the result of progressive cardiac disease stemming from this illness.

Her father, your paternal grandfather, was 6'4", weighed 200 pounds, had graying brown hair, brown eyes, and was healthy and youthful. He worked for many years as a telegrapher.

Your mother had two siblings, a sister—an older sister—and a younger brother.

Your birth father was not seen at the agency and the information we have about him comes from your mother. He was a single Caucasian Protestant man in his early 20's. He was 5'11", weighed 170 pounds, had curly brown hair, a fair complexion and brown eyes and was good looking. He was a high school graduate who was in the Army at the time. He appeared to be in good health although we do not have medical information about him, nor do we know about his family other than the fact that his parents were both alive at the time. He was said to have a pleasant disposition and a good sense of fun.

Your birth parents had a warm, caring relationship but it was not one of permanency. Your mother was caring and conscientious in making a plan for you. She expressed the wish to keep you but knew that her situation did not really allow for this and that adoption could offer you more, with more security, stability and the love of two parents. This was a difficult decision for her to make but she thought it through fully and felt it was the best plan for you.

I do hope that this answers some of your questions and is of benefit to you. If we can be of further help, please do not hesitate to be in touch.

I was stunned by how closely the letter's information supported the facts I had already gathered. The physical characteristics for Barbara May were right on mark, including her height. Barbara May's sister, Nancy, was never that tall. Moreover, Barbara May was working as a secretary in 1952 and, in fact, had had an appendectomy at the age of eleven.

The appendectomy, something I hadn't recalled from the letter, was particularly significant. Nancy even remembered the date of the surgery because it was so unique: 4-4-44.

Nancy and her daughter, Carol, shared letters Barbara May wrote from the hospital while she was recovering from the appendectomy. In one, Barbara May wrote to her aunt, Anastasia, on April 20, 1944. She was still struggling with spelling and grammar:

Dear Annastasia:

How are you, I am feeling fine and my temperature is not high like it was before.

I guess you know I got up today and going home Sat. or Sun. won't that be nice.

My writing is a little better than it was in Grandma's letter because her's was the first I wrote and I was a little shakie.

The reason I want to go home so quick is because in the hospital you have to stay in bed.

I can't wait untill I see the baby chicks...

Mommie called up tonight and said she has everything ready for me when I come home.

Has Bump come home yet? he must be a bad dog when he comes home. You should give him a spanking.

How is Uncle Ed? In the letter he sent he asked me if I snore at night. Mrs. Evans said I don't, so tell him I don't.

I have no more room to write and paper is scarce, so Good-bye.

Love and kisses,
Barbara

Beyond the definitive link to the appendectomy, the letter served as a broader history lesson. The reference to paper scarcity underscored a World War II-related paper shortage, triggered by the use of packaging for military supplies, as well as a military draft that diminished manpower in the lumber industry. In addition, the fact that Barbara May was hospitalized for more than two weeks after the operation highlighted just how far we've come in surgical recoveries; the average length of stay today after an appendectomy is between two and five days. At the time Barbara May wrote the letter to Anastasia, she had been in the hospital for sixteen days.

The description of my mother and the appendectomy reference weren't the only striking details. Of particular note were the descriptions of Barbara May's mother and father—who now appeared to be my grandmother and grandfather. Barbara May's mother, Florence Lawson, was indeed very musical. She also had rheumatic fever as a child and died in her thirties as the result of cardiac disease stemming from the illness; in fact, she died at the age of thirty-nine. Barbara May's father, meanwhile, was in the neighborhood of six-foot-four, two hundred pounds, and was a telegrapher, specifically for the Pennsylvania Railroad. Nancy identified her father as a telegrapher in her eulogy for Barbara May and the 1917 military registration for Nancy and Barbara May's father listed him as a telegraph operator.

Also significant was the mention of my mother's older sister and younger brother, presumably Nancy and Howard.

The reference to German descent was a bit confusing; initially, it didn't seem to be part of my heritage. Later, a revised ancestry.com analysis indicated I did indeed have some German lineage.

The information about my father registered little with me, since no one seemed to know who he was. I did find it interesting that he had served in the military, and I briefly entertained the thought that perhaps he had gone off to war after meeting my mother and was subsequently killed in battle. There was a measure of comfort in that scenario: My father hadn't intentionally abandoned me. My mother had been left in an impossible situation.

Most importantly, I was able to enter surgery with a strong conviction that I had finally found my birth mother—and that may have contributed to my amazingly speedy recovery. I was released home directly from the intensive care unit twenty-four hours after the operation. Modern medicine is indeed spectacular.

So, too, is access to genetic measurement. That was the clincher. Soon after the surgery, Carol's DNA results arrived and her centimorgan count in relation to me was 982, at the high end of the first cousin range. Diane, one of Jeanne's sisters, had also submitted her DNA and it came back at 2,042, at the extremely high end of the grandparent-aunt-uncle-half-sibling range. Again, because of her age and gender, Diane could be nothing else but a half-sibling to me.

The genetic pieces fit the puzzle perfectly. Barbara May was my biological mother.

I wanted to shout the revelation to the mountaintops and may have come close to doing that. I told everyone who would listen, including my newfound relatives. I told my daughter, Amber, and the two sons by my third marriage. I told my wife, Mary, who had patiently listened to me work through the connections over four months. I told J.C., my best friend since elementary school, and several other longtime friends spread out across the country. I told people at work and I mentioned it in passing to journalists at the local ABC-TV affiliate, one of whom was so moved by my journey that he did a short expose on my search titled "A Mother's Love."

I also went back to those first pictures of Barbara May that Carol had sent to me, subsequent pictures of Barbara May's husband, my biological grandfather, grandmother, aunt and half-siblings, and a picture of Barbara May sent by Diane taken just six weeks before Barbara May died.

Looking at the pictures of Barbara May was both thrilling and bittersweet. I again wanted to reach out to her; to feel her touch, to hear her voice, to look into her eyes, to breathe in deeply the essence of her, to love her from a place that only a mother and son could know.

Everyone who is adopted without ever knowing their biological parents has a different experience and a different perspective on the value of searching or not searching. There can be unforeseen, unpleasant consequences in looking for a biological parent.

But one simple thing a person who wasn't adopted can't fully fathom is this: if an adoptee never finds a biological parent or relative, they will always wonder what their parents and relatives look like. They will never be able to sit in a room with a relative and absorb, even unconsciously, similarities of speech, mannerisms and physical appearance. These are things people raised by biological relatives often take for granted, but they can create deep, fundamental bonds that can be formed in no other way.

Barbara May and I will never be able to meet, but at least I now knew it was my birth mother I was looking at in the pictures Carol sent me. I could now tell Barbara May, wherever she was, that I loved her and I could thank her, without reservation, for giving me life.

It was a good start. But there were so many more things I wanted to know.

Barbara May's 1951 senior yearbook photo.

Barbara May in her high school cap and gown.

Above: Barbara May in 1940. Eight years old.

Right: My first visit to Barbara May's grave at Wrightstown, N.J., on May 27, 2017.

| 87

Barbara May in her Easter Sunday best.

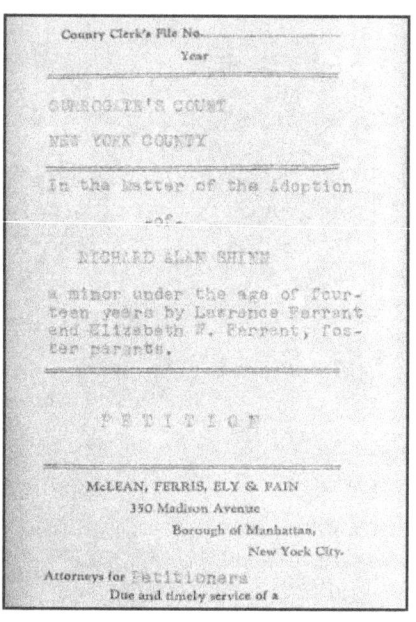

The petition for my adoption and the name (Richard Alan Shinn) that was key to my search.

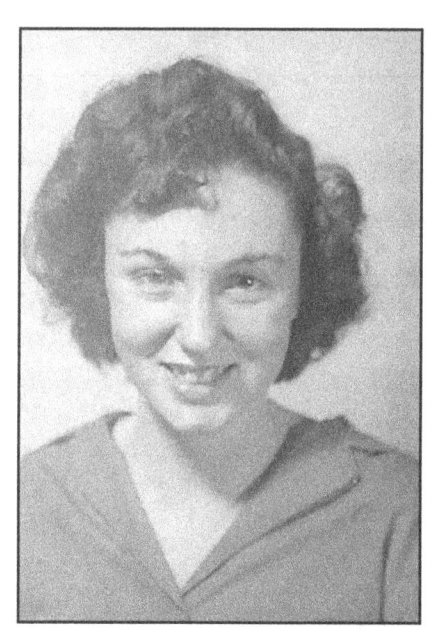

Showing the tousled hair look in 1950.

This photo of Barbara May was taken in April 2005. She died the following month at 73.

Chapter Ten

The exhilaration of finally finding my birth mother came crashing down in late August 2017, barely a month after my surgery. My sixth wife, Mary Hoffman-Farrant, went into a coma and later died. She was sixty-four.

There are several passages in the Bible that, despite my later-in-life take on the forces that define our lives, speak to me in ways that help me soldier on when things get hard. Proverbs 19:21 instructs us, "Many are the plans in the mind of man, but it is the purpose of the Lord that will stand." And Luke 12:48 says, "Everyone to whom much was given, of him much will be required." The first passage, interpreted generally that there is a grand plan designed for each of us, frees me from the belief that I can control everything. The second passage acknowledges the hardships I've endured and encourages me to rise above the burdens.

But the explosion of life-changing events in the four months since the search began left me wondering exactly what kind of grand plan had been designed for me and how much more upheaval was in store. I had traveled from the excitement of discovery to the challenge of surviving surgery to the seemingly bottomless depths of despair and emptiness associated with loss. Enough, I thought. Seriously. Enough.

Mary's descent to death took just nine days, but the course of her demise was cemented long before that. She was an alcoholic. She never acknowledged her addiction, at least not publicly, but she had been drinking regularly, sometimes heavily, for most of her adult life. Her first marriage, which lasted twenty-three years, ended in 1998 after she refused a treatment plan during a family intervention—a fact I learned after her death. In the years between her divorce and our first meeting in 2007, she continued drinking and kept the company of others with the same disease. I didn't fully recognize her addiction until after we married in 2009, and I spent our entire marriage trying to coax her into quitting, or at least getting some help. Each time, I was met with denial and dismissiveness.

My adoptive mother was an admitted alcoholic, so I feel I should have recognized it earlier in Mary. I used to detest my mother's syrupy demeanor after she'd had a few glasses of brandy or wine every night after work. Wine was also Mary's choice of destruction, and I would find empty bottles of the stuff under beds, under an ottoman, or tucked into the far recesses of a closet. She, too, was an overly friendly drunk. I came to wonder if, through Mary, I was trying to re-write a script.

Although Mary's drinking caused friction in our relationship, she was otherwise a wonderful, beautiful person of good humor, uplifting spirit, and with a generosity that extended to many except herself. She did not take care of herself, avoiding doctors at almost any cost, and she was prone to falling despite her athleticism early in life.

Much of Mary's caring was reserved for the multitude of animals she took in over the years. She had never had children, so she considered her animals her kids and frequently referred to herself as their mom. Each time she left our Fort Wayne condominium, she would tell her animals, "Mom will be home soon. It won't be long." When she died, she left behind, and entrusted to me, a friendly golden retriever and five spoiled cats of varying heritages.

It's hard to reconcile the rest of her life with her propensity for alcohol. In pictures taken during her high school years, when she was the lead cheerleader, she looked gorgeous, ebullient, and thoroughly happy. Later, she and her high school sweetheart and eventual husband co-owned a successful retail business, where her talents as a jewelry designer, store display manager and buyer helped the business prosper. She was also a pretty handy basket-weaver.

By the time I met her, she was still talented and attractive with an effusive personality. But she had become utterly irresponsible financially. She had borrowed heavily against the condominium mortgage and was woefully behind in her mortgage and homeowners association fees. She had also let the condition of the condominium deteriorate, and while we were dating, her car was repossessed when she fell behind in payments.

I helped her settle her debts, almost to the exclusion of attending to my own. At least once a month, I also tried to have discussions with her about her drinking, alternating between gentle, middling and stern. In the end, I took control of all of the finances to protect us. And I never stopped trying to encourage her to stop drinking.

I'm not sure I will ever be able to pinpoint the cause of Mary's alcoholism. Perhaps she never got over the death of her mother, Gloria, who succumbed to cancer at the age of thirty-nine in 1966 when Mary was just thirteen and her sister Nancy was ten—a circumstance eerily similar to the death of Barbara May's mother. Perhaps Mary never got over the failure of her first marriage. Perhaps it was a combination of things. Maybe there was no external trigger at all; that her biological makeup made her predisposed to addiction.

Whatever the case, her drinking caught up with her in a big way in early 2017 when she was diagnosed with cirrhosis of the liver, a frequent consequence of alcoholism. Her skin seemed to age overnight, her belly swelled with fluid, and she grew lethargic. She continued working as a regional sales representative for an international wholesale gift distributor, but often when she got home from work, she would lie down and take long naps. Twice she had enormous amounts of fluid extracted from her abdomen. The third time, when fluid was also detected around one of her lungs, doctors suggested putting her on a liver transplant list. They also said that her kidneys were exhibiting signs of stress and that dialysis might be in her future.

The evening after the third fluid extraction—August 24, 2017, a Wednesday—I visited Mary at the hospital. She was scheduled to be released the following day, and although the prospect of a liver transplant posed a significant challenge, we shared a mostly uneventful couple of hours. She ordered cheesecake for the two of us, something we both enjoyed. We watched the news on TV. And we briefly discussed the latest health hurdle; briefly, because Mary never liked discussing her own health. I began the conversation delicately:

"So what do you think about all of this?" I asked.

"All of what?"

"The health stuff. The liver transplant."

She paused. "I think I should be getting a will."

"I suppose that's a good idea," I said. "But honey, you're going to need to adopt a warrior spirit about this. We need to fight this thing."

She did not respond to my pleading. But her remark about a will was the first indication that she acknowledged the seriousness of her condition. For Mary, that recognition was a major breakthrough.

I left her with a series of written questions to ask the doctors at the hospital. What is the next step regarding a liver transplant? At what point will we know if dialysis is necessary? What is the stage of the liver cirrhosis and what is the short- and long-term prognosis? Why are the kidneys suddenly experiencing problems? And can't the fluid in her abdomen be removed before such large build-ups? Weeks later, I found the list of questions in her pink bag. I will never know if she sought the answers.

The day after I spent time with Mary at the hospital, her sister, who had driven to Fort Wayne from South Bend, took her back to the condominium. By the time I arrived home from work, Mary was sleeping in our bed and I had no intention of waking her. Her sister returned to South Bend, I eventually went to sleep beside Mary, and sometime in the middle of the night she got up and went back to sleep in the spare bedroom.

When I prepared to leave for work on the morning of August 26, 2017, a Friday, I did what I always did. I announced from the bedroom entrance that I was leaving. Mary would invariably ask me what time it was, I would tell her, and she would either let me know that she, too, needed to get up or that she would snooze for another fifteen minutes or so. But on this morning, her response was a stark "What do you want?" It was an odd remark and so I repeated that I was leaving for work. "What do you want?" she said again.

She had the covers pulled up around her head and she was facing away from me. I decided not to bother her, figuring she might still be groggy from her latest fluid extraction. But her response was completely out of character, and I called work to say I would be late coming in so I could monitor Mary's condition.

An hour later, while I was in another room, I heard Mary shrieking "Stop it! Stop It! Stop It!" and I raced to the bedroom. I found her standing in the middle of the room looking straight ahead, unfocused and terribly incontinent. I spoke soothingly to her while I cleaned her up and struggled to get her back into bed.

She was physically combative and incapable of carrying on a meaningful two-way conversation. At one point, trying to assess her level of cognition, I asked her what my name was. "Rick!" she screamed, as if annoyed by my query. She was clearly not in her right mind.

I called her family physician and a nurse instructed me to get her to the emergency room. The nurse suggested Mary might be experiencing an imbalance of electrolytes, but her condition, it would become apparent, was far worse.

The fragility of my healing incisions from the aortic surgery prevented me from picking Mary up and taking her to the car, so I tried gently to encourage her to get out of bed. She fought me at every turn.

"Mary," I said, lightly tugging at her wrists, "I need you to get up."

"Okay," she said, and then promptly wrested her arms away from me and collapsed back on the bed.

"Mary, I need you to get up."

"Okay," she said from her prone position. But she didn't move.

Eventually, I was able to get her to sit up, but she refused to stand, flailing at me every time I tried to ease her up. So I sought reinforcement, called her sister in South Bend and put her on the speaker phone.

"Mary," her sister said, "you need to go with Rick to the emergency room."

"What do you want?" Mary said.

"You need to go with Rick."

"What do you want?"

"Do you want me to come down there?" her sister asked.

Mary was silent.

"Mary," I said, "Your sister wants to know if you want her to come here."

Silence.

"Mary, do you want me to come down?" her sister asked.

Mary paused for a long time, trying to unscramble her brain. Finally, she answered in a low voice, almost a whisper: "Yes."

Getting Mary to the car was a monumental ordeal once she was upright. Holding her by the wrists and walking backward, I repeated over and over in rhythm: "Good girl, good girl. Great job, great job. You're doing great, honey. Good girl, good girl. Great job, great job." Occasionally she would stop. Throughout she protested. "God damn you!" she yelled. "God damn you!"

When I finally got her to the car, and after several minutes managed to nudge her into the passenger seat, I heard the last words I would ever hear from my wife: "You're a fucking asshole!"

For the entire trip to the hospital, she remained quiet, slouched in the seat beside me. When we arrived at the entrance to the emergency room, it took four people to remove her from the car as she grumbled and flailed. A short time later, she began to slip into a coma.

Only once during that horrible morning in the condo did I witness the compassionate Mary I knew. As I was leading her from the bedroom, she stopped at one point, lifted her right palm to my chest, and tenderly placed it there for several seconds. She said nothing, but in that moment it was as if she were saying, "I love you. I'm not okay. Please help me."

I would soon learn that what Mary was experiencing was a condition called hepatic encephalopathy, caused in her case by dangerously high levels of ammonia in her brain—ammonia that her damaged liver was no longer filtering from her system. The goal in the hospital ICU, the gastroenterologist and the attending physician explained to me, would be to get the ammonia level down through a combination of treatments. If it could be reduced to a normal or near-normal level, there was a chance she would wake up. "Let's give it until Thursday," the liver doctor told me that weekend. "Let's see where we're at then."

We waited by her bedside—me, her sister, her sister's husband, and one of her sister's daughters. We spent hours in the ICU, monitoring the blood tests, hoping beyond hope, and listening to the gradually fading rhythm of her breathing. When Mary grew agitated, she was given sedatives intravenously. When her raspy breathing stopped for what seemed like interminable periods, we sat on the edge of our chairs, wondering if she would take another breath.

On the chance that she could hear us, we told her we loved her and encouraged her to keep fighting. Over and over, I kissed her forehead and stroked her hair. Away from her, we all cried tears born of immeasurable fear and pain.

By Monday, her ammonia levels had been reduced to near normal. She remained in a coma, but we were briefly buoyed and we told her it was time to awaken. By Tuesday, the levels rose again, even with medical intervention, and we told her it was okay to let go. By Wednesday, the levels had more than doubled, and I was summoned to a small room at the hospital, where doctors and nurses delivered the news that they had done all they could and that hospice care was probably the best option. I looked into their faces searching for even the slightest sign of wavering, I asked dozens of questions hoping for some hint of hope, and finally I asked the attending physician, whom I had come to trust, what he would do if it was one of his loved ones in the same condition. He gave me the answer I did not want to hear but knew intuitively was the only answer. Hospice.

I had wanted to give Mary a fighting chance and now we had reached the point where the fight was ostensibly over. She was losing ground and nothing the doctors were doing would pull her out of the coma. Consenting to send her to hospice that day was the right thing to do, but I felt I was giving up on the person to whom I had pledged unfailing support. Although it was her liver that was killing her, I felt like I was the one handing her the death sentence.

At the hospice facility, I told her several times that it was okay to go. Twenty-three years earlier, I had done the same thing when my adoptive mother was dying of bone cancer and receiving hospice care at home in Pound Ridge. Three days before she died, I called the hospice nurse from my home in Illinois for an update and asked her to put the phone up to my mother's ear. The nurse cautioned me that my mother hadn't uttered a word for days and was essentially comatose. Nevertheless, I spoke to my mother, telling her it was okay to go, that she had been a good mother, that I would be alright, and that I loved her. I was startled when she responded in a clear voice. "I love you," she said. They were the last words she would ever utter.

Mary lasted three days in hospice care. Her breathing became more erratic, phlegm and blood began oozing from her mouth, and her arms and legs grew still. The night before she died—a Friday—we left hospice to try and get some sleep. We were beyond exhausted and nearly out of our minds. The next morning, I arrived at hospice at 8:50 A.M., walked into her room, and I knew beyond any doubt that the end was near. Her breathing was shallow and punctuated by long periods of no breath at all. She was shutting down. She was nearly gone.

I kissed her forehead, stroked her hair and then, holding her head in my hands, I told her, "This is goodbye, honey. You put up a good fight. I love you, honey. I will always love you."

I returned to my car in the parking lot to collect myself and wait for her family members to arrive. Twenty-two minutes later, at 9:12 A.M. on September 2, 2017, she took her last breath. One of the hospice nurses crossed the parking lot to my car, I rolled down the window, and the nurse said softly, "She has passed."

I can't be certain, but I think Mary had been waiting for me that morning.

Chapter Eleven

Stripped to its searing essence, there are few elegant ways to describe grief. It just sucks.

In the days leading up to Mary's death and the days afterward, I was immersed in a swirling cloud of irrationality. One part of my brain was laser-focused on the perfunctory tasks that needed to be done. Another was lost in a meandering series of impulses that were bereft of logic.

Everywhere I drove, I was keenly aware of parents dropping their children off at school, people slipping in and out of stores, and couples walking hand in hand down sidewalks. They were all part of the routine of a normal life and I wanted to shout from the window of the car: "Don't you know what's going on? Don't you know about Mary?" It was inconceivable to me that life could go on for others. What I wanted was for the world to stop and take notice, not only of Mary's death, but of my grief.

Similar thoughts haunted me in moments alone at home. As I sat outside our sunroom, I thought, "How is it that the sun is still shining, the leaves are still lilting in the wind, and the birds are still singing? How is it that Mary's dog and cats still need to be fed and nurtured, that the bills still need to be paid, that the grocery runs still need to be made, and that I still need to go to work?"

In the small bit of sanity I had left, I knew it would be dangerous to dwell on such thoughts and impulses for too long. So I tried to put myself in situations where I could move forward, even though in my heart I didn't want to carry on, and even though, suddenly, I understood why some people who lose loved ones lose the will to live. They are the ones who die a short time later of a broken heart, or take their own lives, or remain forever stuck in a bleak rote-like procession of drudgeries.

Those options scared me to the core, so the night after Mary died, I ventured forty minutes to the lake home of friends, sat around a camp fire with them, talked about subjects far removed from my gloom, and slept in a pitch-black room that was a welcomed escape from the world. The next night, after a long, lonely Labor Day, I drove through a pelting rain to see *The Glass Castle* in a 261-seat theater that, but for me, was literally empty. Somehow that seemed appropriate. I had been granted the gift of a private space to laugh, cry, and grieve.

I avoided looking at pictures of Mary, avoided being alone for too long, and didn't listen to her voicemails still stored in my phone, except for one—the last message she sent, two days before she slipped into a coma. It was an ordinary update from the hospital where her physician, after seeing her in an outpatient setting, had admitted her to have the fluid removed from her abdomen and determine if other serious things were going on internally:

> Hey, I'm at, um, Dupont (Hospital). They're going to run some blood work on me and if possible they're gonna get rid of my stomach bloat. Because that's apparently what's causing all of this discomfort with the breathing and the walking. It's all related. So I will let you know what's going on. They're gonna try and do it yet today, but I don't know. I'll let you know. Bye.

We both knew that the fluid buildup had been making it difficult for her to breathe and walk, so it was strange that she felt that was important to tell me. But there was more to it, and that evening she revealed the full story as we shared cheesecake in her hospital room. Fluid, she said, had built up around one of her lungs and her kidneys were showing signs of stress.

Mary sounded tired and disconnected in the final voicemail, and what really hit home was how we tend to move through our lives under the assumption that there will be another day, another chance to engage in more meaningful ways with the ones we love. That we often don't regularly tell those closest to us how important they are to us, how much we love them, and how eager we are to see them again.

In my life, I have been guilty of taking such things for granted, and after listening to the voicemail, I recommitted myself to doing a better job of expressing appreciation to others.

I also busied myself with a host of necessary tasks: writing her obituary, which noted private services would be held later in her native Canada; letting her friends and acquaintances know of her passing; making arrangements for her cremation; helping plan an October celebration of her life in the sweeping meadow behind our Fort Wayne condo; carting her death notice around to accounts that required name changes; beginning to look for homes for some of the animals (because six was too overwhelming); going to work, which was a great distraction, and crying in all the tortured moments in between.

Her sister made the bulk of the arrangements for the celebration of life, securing the tent, the finger food, the flowers, and creating photo boards memorializing Mary's life. She also ordered a cake with the words "Until We Meet Again." I, meanwhile, ordered balloons in two shades of pink—Mary's favorite color—and wrote the eulogy. I almost didn't make it through it:

> Thank you all for coming today. Mary, I'm sure, is looking down and smiling.
>
> This place, this meadow, was one of Mary's favorite places. This and the towpath just a short distance through those woods.
>
> Mary loved looking out on this meadow and seeing the rich greens of spring and summer, the changing of the colors in the fall, and the snow-laden trees in winter. She watched the birds that flocked to the feeders, occasionally she'd spot deer crossing the very spot where we now stand, and she delighted in throwing balls into the meadow for Molly, her beloved golden retriever. Animals were her greatest joy and, in her absence, the dog and cats she left behind mourn and search for a new normal, as I do.
>
> We never talked about where her final ceremony would be held—in fact both of us thought I would go first, given my medical history. But what she did want was a gathering of people with

whom she shared her life and a celebration of happy memories. And I certainly have many of those. She was my love, my partner, and my most ardent cheerleader. She was committed to bringing good cheer to everyone she met, she cared about others more than she cared for herself, and with her good humor, her penchant for bright colors, and her playful demeanor she brought joy to the world.

We cried together at movies, we matched wits with 'Jeopardy,' and every so often, as a treat to ourselves, we'd go to Zesto's for chocolate malts. She picked out my clothes—and on that score I'm really screwed now. She listened to me playing the guitar and occasionally joined in on choruses, never mind that she would sing out of key. She delighted in my recent search for my birth mother and she had me read chapters of a book I'm writing about that search.

Mary did not feel well the last year of her life, but she soldiered on, working extraordinarily hard in her job, continuing to foster a giving spirit, and fighting mightily against the disease that would claim her. She was a warrior who rarely complained.

I don't think Mary ever realized how many lives she touched and I certainly don't think she realized how important she was to my life. She would often say, "You would be fine without me." But that couldn't have been further from the truth. I miss her smile. I miss her caring heart. I miss her love of sunflowers, bunny rabbits, the color pink, and muffins. She was, honest to God, always bringing home muffins. As if muffins made a meal.

I am grateful that Mary and I had a few special moments in the months before she died, including a week spent at a darling little cabin in Michigan in July. She had picked the cabin and she was thoroughly happy that week. And it was during that week that we made an enduring memory I will never forget. We went kayaking on a meandering river leading to Lake Michigan. I did most of the paddling that day; Mary's strength was fading. But it was a beautiful day, the water was stunningly placid, and Mary sat in the front of the kayak taking in the lush marshes, the ducks and the geese, and the gentle breezes that crossed our way. She was truly at peace out there on the water. And now she has found peace again—an everlasting peace.

To know Mary, especially when she was at her best, was to catch a sparkling beacon of multi-colored light. And what she would want for us is to take that light and share it with others. To make the most of our time on earth and fill our lives—and the lives of others—with the colors of joy, hope and love.

A little bit later, we will symbolically recognize that wish and give Mary a send-off with the pink balloons you see here today. That is one thing she and I did talk about. She wanted pink balloons sent aloft. And I gave her my promise we would do just that.

I took out my guitar and sang James Taylor's "Country Road," a song Mary had heard me play dozens of times. Friends, family, her ex-husband, and former work colleagues then chimed in with stories about Mary, some of them serious, some of them humorous, all of them heartfelt. The celebration of life ended with a balloon launch that defied the elements and was rich with symbolism.

From all appearances, the light breeze that day seemed to be blowing west to east, and toward a tall, ominous stand of trees waiting to pop a balloon or two. But we carried on, and I signaled the balloon release with these words: "This is for you, Mary. May you forever fly free." The mourners, each holding a single balloon, then let go and, inexplicably, the balloons rose over the condo and headed not east toward the trees, but due north, toward Canada. She was going home.

When the ceremony was over, I called my cousin, Carol, who had become my rock in the storm. We talked by phone almost every day, sometimes for hours. In addition to sharing pictures of my newfound relatives, she provided essential support by offering words of comfort; perspectives about life and death; advice on how to maneuver through the labyrinth of emotions connected to the death of a loved one; quotes about grief, as well as wisdom she had gained from the death of her father and her innate sense of the human experience that had served her well for many years as a New Jersey schoolteacher. She had become a very good friend, even though we had never met, and we delighted in the knowledge that for a brief time, there had been the possibility we were half-siblings. She called me her "pretend brother." I called her my "pretend sister."

On the day of the celebration of life—a Saturday—Carol wrote this email to me:

> Hi Rick:
>
> As I write this email, I hope you are getting some sleep. I know it's been a crummy day for you and Sunday will probably be just as difficult. I wish there was something I could say or do to make the heartache go away but we both know that this is all part of the grieving process. Sometimes you'll take steps forward and many times you'll be heading backwards. There is no right or wrong way to deal with the loss of a loved one. Everyone feels grief in different ways. Quite often grief is like living two lives... one where you pretend that everything is going to be just fine and another where your heart is screaming in pain because you loved so much. I recently saw a quote that said, "Grief only exists where love lived first." When we take the risk of love, we often have to experience great loss because we loved first. Although it's easy for our heads to rationalize that, it's not as easy for our hearts to grasp that concept.
>
> So...take the time that you need to mourn the loss of Mary. No one guarantees that it won't be painful, especially as this is still all very new for you. There will be unexpected things that open the floodgates of tears and that's okay. Go easy on yourself and try not to beat yourself up for wondering about the "what ifs" or "maybes." We all know the past can't be changed. Just know that you did all you could to help your beautiful wife and you obviously loved her unconditionally. I'm sure you provided great happiness for her while you were together.
>
> I know I'm babbling right now, but I wanted to send a quick email before I head to bed. I'll end with the following:

On this roller coaster of grief, just know that there are many who care (including me). You know that I'm only a phone call away when you need to talk.

Hang in there and be good to yourself!
Hugs,
Carol

I was also supported by almost constant, compassionate communication from the CEO of Easter Seals Arc of Northeast Indiana, where I served as a board member. It was a source of great comfort that the CEO took time out of her busy personal and professional life to make sure I was not slogging through the grief process alone. Others, too, including J.C., my best friend in childhood, reached out periodically with sympathy and offers to help in any way they could.

Of all the things I read and heard about grief, friendly overtures notwithstanding, one notion got me through the days and nights: grief is not something you get over. It is something you learn to live with. It has become a part of my being, whether I like it or not, and I don't have to look for it. It will always find me, even without prodding. In the shower. While driving to work. When passing by a restaurant where Mary and I once dined together.

And so, I accepted grief as part of a process that was neither a product of my making nor something I could control—and gradually the intensity of the loss dulled.

There was a fall Sunday morning in mid-October when I began to sense that I could find beauty and peace in a life without Mary. I took Molly for a walk along the nearby towpath, a walk Molly, Mary, and I had taken many times. The path intermittingly follows the hollow of the long-abandoned Wabash and Erie Canal, carved out in the 1830s and 1840s, and once considered the premier mode of cross-country travel and trade before the railroads emerged full force. The trail was another of Mary's favorite places.

That Sunday morning, in the warm blanket of the sun across my shoulders and the rustle of the turning leaves, I both yearned for Mary and welcomed newness. The world was alive again, crisp and begging earnest exploration—for the living, for those of us still here. And it became clear to me that life is meant to be inhaled with great vigor, no matter the inevitable hurdles. Every moment, every experience is essential to our constant re-creation of ourselves.

I chose fairly quickly after Mary's death to lean into life and life, even without Mary, moved on.

Condo neighbors planted a little magnolia tree at the edge of the meadow in Mary's honor. Mary's sister retired from her alumni office job at the University of Notre Dame. One of Mary's beloved nieces got engaged to her longtime boyfriend. The shuttered high school where Mary starred as a cheerleader was targeted for demolition. The dog and two of the cats were adopted into new homes. And I went searching for my next chapter.

Grief will always be a part of me, but it will neither define nor defeat me. It will simply be another layer of my existence, absorbed, accepted and, in the end, complementing the many shades of my humanity.

Chapter Twelve

Another person was in my corner in the wake of Mary's death, someone who's always had my back: my adopted daughter, Amber.

Some special reckoning was going on when an adult adoptee fighting feelings of abandonment and rejection found himself paired with a little girl whose biological father had abandoned her.

Amber was four years old when I met her mother, and I was instantly taken by Amber's spirit. Unbearably cute, smart, energetic, trusting and hopeful, she became, in a matter of weeks, a daddy's girl, following me everywhere and entrusting to me both her dreams and her confusion about why her biological father never saw or contacted her. Although our circumstances were different, the resulting feelings of confusion and abandonment were similar. I felt uniquely suited to help Amber manage her pain.

I didn't know at the time that my biological mother had struggled with giving me up for adoption, so I was able to talk with Amber from a place of feeling utterly cast out as a child. I suggested ways she could think about her situation that, if it didn't completely mask the hurt, would at least allow her to move forward in a positive way. I could not only empathize with her, but guide her.

Amber had known her father for a short time while she, her father, and her mother, whom I would later marry, lived in Arizona. But when the relationship between her parents broke up, Amber and her mother returned to her mother's hometown of Danville, Illinois, where I worked as the managing editor of the daily newspaper. Eventually, communication between Amber and her father, who paid no child support, drifted into silence.

To help mitigate her confusion and grief, I shared with Amber what I had told myself over the years about my biological mother: that her father's disinterest was not a reflection of her value, that it should not define her present or her future, and that she was an amazing person. I also told her that her father's inability to interact with her was the result of his own character flaws and that it was his loss that he had chosen to disappear from her life.

For the most part, our talks seemed to comfort Amber in the short term, but it was impossible for her to not wonder why her father seemed disinterested. For years, she harbored the thought of calling her father. Both her mother and I recommended against it early on, worried that she would not be strong enough to handle what almost certainly would be more rejection. But after she turned eight, we relented. We had just two notes of caution for her: do not expect that the phone call will make a difference, and do not forget that you are terrific.

The call did not last long and one particular exchange told Amber all she needed to know. She asked her father why he hadn't sent her cards and presents for Christmases and birthdays. Her father said, "Why don't you send me those things?" Amber knew immediately, perhaps because of our discussions, how wrong that response was—that it is the parent's responsibility, not the child's, to lead by example.

Shortly after that phone call, we asked Amber if she thought it would be okay if I adopted her, and she was thrilled with the idea. As a courtesy, we called her father to make sure he had no problem with me adopting Amber. That was the second big hurt. Her father didn't express even the slightest reservation. "How," Amber asked me, "can a father so easily give up his child?"

The answer to a question like that isn't simple, because any decent parent would have a hard time letting go of a child. I told her I didn't know how a father could do that.

"But what I do know, Amber," I said, "is that he is missing out on knowing one of the most incredible people on the face of the earth, and I will be more than thrilled and proud to officially call you my daughter."

Then I told her I loved her, using the nickname I still call her today: Amberific.

She, in turn, calls me "Pops" or "Sir, O Great One." The latter is an inside joke stemming from an impromptu request I once made that must've come from a somewhat demented mind. She was four or five years old and we were standing in the checkout line of a grocery store. Like most young children, she asked if she could have candy. Frustrated by endless, unsuccessful efforts to curb such behavior, I said, "If you call me 'Sir, O Great One,' you can have a candy bar." I have no idea where that came from, but I was convinced she wouldn't do it. I was wrong. For years after that, and likely to the horror of other shoppers, she would call me "Sir, O Great One" whenever she wanted something in the checkout line. Fortunately, it seemed to have no damaging effect on her personal growth.

Amber is today a well-adjusted woman, a graduate of the University of North Carolina-Charlotte, and pursuing a career in that state. She is a hard worker, a person of integrity and common sense, compassionate to a fault, and our love for each other is stronger with each passing year. And while I imagine she may think about her now-deceased father from time to time, we rarely discuss him, and I am fairly confident she is secure in her own self-worth.

One of her greatest gifts to me is that she has loved me without judgment, even as I drifted through relationships and marriages after her mother and I divorced. She has told me more than once, "I just want you to be happy." She means it. I hope I have been equally supportive of her. I think I have.

Like most children, she had her teenage moments, but they were hardly problematic. She furiously stomped her feet up the stairs whenever I insisted she clean her room. She really hated cleaning her room. And when I would rock out to music on the car radio, she would slide off her seat to the floor and hide.

"Dad, people are watching!"

"No one's watching, Amber," I'd say.

"Yes they are, Dad. I'm serious, Dad. You better stop it!"

I'm sure my laughter didn't help.

Amber has long since forgiven me for such despicable parental behaviors and has been there for me during the most difficult times in my life, including my surgery to repair the aortic aneurysm. I can always count on her to be by my side. I, in turn, will always be there for her whenever she needs me.

We understand each other. We love each other unconditionally. And in no small way, some of the credit for that bond is due to Barbara May.

Had I not been adopted, had I not lived without answers about my biological mother, and had I not struggled to find purpose and identity, it might have been harder for me to fully relate to Amber's situation and help her.

It's nothing short of amazing how our lives perfectly aligned.

Chapter Thirteen

I was never the biggest Bruce Springsteen fan, but it was interesting to learn that the legendary rocker grew up in Freehold, New Jersey, and was, apparently like Barbara May, somewhat of a nonconformist. The two may have even known each other.

Barbara May told one of her daughters that she had been Bruce's babysitter at one point, but I could never confirm that with his representatives; that is, they never responded to my inquiries. Real or not, though, it makes for an interesting tidbit. It is equally intriguing that my biological roots, like Springsteen's, are firmly planted in the working class.

I learned of my geographical connection to The Boss on my second trip to Monmouth County, which I had planned before Mary took ill. The plane tickets had been purchased, the hotel room reserved, and the itinerary settled with Barbara May's nieces, Carol and Susan, and Barbara May's sister, Nancy. I boarded the plane just three weeks after Mary's passing.

I was still searching for my new normal, first after the discovery of Barbara May, and then after Mary's death. I was no longer even remotely in control of my life's path and it was everything I could do to function. Work provided a distraction from the swirl of events around me, but it was also a challenge. As the communications director for northeast Indiana's workforce development organization, I promoted and helped provide strategy for adult and youth education and training programs, job search assistance, and employer engagement.

For four years in that role, I was consumed by a passionate devotion to helping other people improve their lives. Now, I found myself struggling to keep my own ship afloat.

I'm sure I had a perpetual deer-in-the-headlights look, and a part of me felt like I was dishonoring Mary's memory by flying off to New Jersey. But I also believed that Mary, who had taken such great interest in my search, would have said, "You go. Really. You go." And so I went.

I flew into Newark, rented a car, drove to Freehold, and met Carol and Nancy at the Methodist church where, four months earlier, I had sat in a pew and observed Carol sitting to my right—my first live view of a biological relative. On my second trip, we exited our cars in the church parking lot and politely exchanged hugs—the first time I had ever touched a biological relative.

In the sanctuary, we had an unexpected meeting with the church's pastor, the Reverend Loraine Priestley-Smith, after we had gone inside to notify someone that my rental car would be parked in the church lot for a few hours. The pastor, who had been working on her Sunday sermon, was so moved by our story of family unification that she delivered a powerful private prayer for the three of us. She then offered her hunch on why God had allowed so many dramatic things to happen to me in such a short time: God knew, she said, that Mary would die soon and leave a hole in my heart. Instead of having two holes in my heart—Mary and Barbara May—He gave me Barbara May and other members of my biological family. In doing so, and also in ensuring I survive the surgery, He also answered a concern of Nancy's that her two daughters would be left without someone to lean on when she died. That person, the pastor said, would be me.

Carol and Susan are strong, independent women and I'm not sure I will be desperately needed to prop them up when Nancy passes. And the hole in the heart theory is intriguing if not a bit contrived-sounding. Nevertheless, all three of us walked out of the church feeling comforted and somewhat awe-struck by the possibility that the pastor just may have been right. Some truly unusual forces seemed to be at play.

That church, its pastor, and the congregation will always have a special place in my heart. They welcomed me warmly on the first visit (especially two sweet elderly parishioners named Annabel and Ruth) when no one in the church knew me. Even in my absence after that, Carol, who is the church's financial secretary, made sure people learned about me and I was added to the church's prayer chain.

Despite my distaste for organized religion, I discovered with the First United Methodist Church of Freehold that there are places where a genuine, non-judgmental love of strangers dwells and where, I suspect, being a good Christian isn't just practiced on Sundays. Certainly, my experience with the church in Freehold was decidedly different from my time attending the Pound Ridge Community Church, another historic white church steeped in the United Methodist tradition. I attended that church regularly with my adoptive parents, but the atmosphere never felt warm and inviting, and for my parents, showing up every Sunday was clearly for show—to give the impression that we were a happy, virtuous family united in Christ. The reality is that the teachings of the Bible were literally never discussed in our home and rarely practiced. As a result, I never felt comforted as a child, and only occasionally as an adult, by the traditional notion of a God, although I am wholly supportive of others who find solace in this belief. It is tempting, given how hard this life is, to believe in a single supreme entity deciding our destinies. It makes the unexplainable more readily explainable. I think, though, it's more complicated than that.

The generosity of churchgoers wasn't the only discovery during my second trip to Freehold. Carol drove us past Springsteen's former childhood home at 39½ Institute Street, a modest, half-shotgun house that Springsteen described in his book "Born To Run" as having four tiny rooms and no hot water. We also ate at Springsteen's favorite pizza joint, Federici's Family Restaurant. The owner told us Springsteen had been in the restaurant a few weeks earlier with a party of more than two dozen.

The rest of the visit was devoted to learning about my biological family, including hours sitting at Carol's large kitchen island poring over an enormous, ornately-covered family scrapbook that read: "Lawson Family Album. Photographs and Memorabilia Compiled by Anastasia L. Brockway." Barbara May's aunt, it seemed, had saved everything, including photographs and letters dating back generations, and even Barbara May's birth announcement sent out on little "stork telegraphs" by her mother, Florence. The announcements were titled "Sweet-egrams" and read:

Arrived: 11:20 p.m. on May 27, 1932
Weighed in at 8½ pounds
Mother getting along fine.
Name: Barbara

There was also another letter from Barbara May, this one to her grandmother after getting home from her appendectomy in 1944. In it, Barbara May talks about feeling a little better, mentions all the gifts she got in the hospital, and expresses gratitude that her sister and father had brought her more baby chickens to raise. "I still got big chickens," Barbara May wrote, "so counting them all together I have 21 chickens."

The scrapbook also included a letter to Barbara May from her mom when Florence was in the hospital. That letter is postmarked Sept. 17, 1945, just twenty-seven days before Florence's death on Oct. 13, 1945. The letter, on paper framed by a dotted green, red and blue border, reads:

Dear Barbara,

> How is school coming along? I wish you could write about it and I'd like it very much if you would make the Safety Patrol this year again…
>
> I am enclosing a dollar for which I'd like you to mail me a book of 3-cent postage stamps and see if you can get me a new deck of playing cards and also if possible, those Peppermint coated chewing gum, also the Freehold Transcript.
>
> How do you like my writing paper? Aunt Lenora sent it to me and I'm writing to her to-night to thank her.
>
> Dr. Appleton said he saw you in Farmingdale Friday riding your bicycle. He told one of the nurses here that you liked children so much that you were going to have eleven (11) children when you got married.
>
> There is a baby boy here, 3 months old, his mother left him here when he was born and said she'd be back and get him and she never did, so the little boy is up for adoption. The nurses tell me there are so many who want him, he is so cute.

Dr. Appleton wanted to know how Peck's bad boy is (he means Howard). Tell Howard to write to me. He said he would. How is Aunt Elsie? Is she really mad at you or do you imagine she is?

Anyhow, be a good girl, take care of Howard for me and make him go to bed the same time as I do—9 p.m.

Love and kisses,
Mommie

Did you get your sneakers yet? Daddy said he'd been trying so hard. Hope you have luck.

I can't help but wonder if the story about the little boy being put up for adoption didn't come back to Barbara May seven years later when she gave birth to me. Perhaps the fact so many wanted him made it just a little easier for Barbara May to give me up for adoption.

In another letter two days later to Anastasia (Florence called her "Stash"), Barbara May's mother wrote about the expense of her hospital stay, opined that she could just as easily be given medicine for her rheumatism at home, complained that she was "stopped up" because something was wrong with her plumbing, and lamented at how noisy the hospital was. She wrote: "There's a lady dying in the next room and another one vomits just at meal time and another one keeps saying, 'Oh! Oh! Oh! Oh!' So it's not quiet here at all."

In an earlier letter to her mother and Anastasia in Toms River, New Jersey, in 1944, Florence described how the rheumatism was making her joints lock up, mentioned that Nancy had designed an award-winning Red Cross poster and that Barbara May was not doing particularly well in school because she was doing "too much fooling in class," and asked her mother to "remember me to anyone who happens to make you a visit."

Among the other items in the scrapbook were Barbara May's eighth grade commencement program from Howell Township School on June 11, 1947 and her high school graduation commencement program from Freehold High School on June 15, 1951. For Freehold High, it was the seventy-fifth annual commencement.

There was also a short note from Harold Page Shinn Sr., Barbara May's father, dated 1958. It's not clear to whom the letter was written. It was written in Spanish, mailed from Havana, Cuba, and accompanied by a blurry black-and-white photograph of him standing in front of palms and a semi-circular section of the majestic National Capital Building (El Capitolio). He is wearing what looks like a straw fedora, white pants, a striped shirt, and round glasses. His hands are firmly planted in his pockets and from what I can make out, he bears a striking resemblance to me in my sixties. He would have been about sixty-three.

The note accompanying the photograph translates to: "Again, I am free and life here is good. That's the truth. I am very content."

I have no idea what the reference to "free" means, and he made no reference to the Cuban Revolution, which ultimately brought Fidel Castro to power. The year before Harold Page Shinn's 1958 letter, revolutionaries attempted to assassinate Cuban President Fulgencio Batista. Then in 1958, Castro's forces and other resistance groups took over numerous towns and provinces. On January 1, 1959, Batista fled Cuba for the Dominican Republic. A year later, Ernest Hemingway, who wrote "The Old Man and the Sea" in Cuba and had it published the year I was born, fled to Ketchum, Idaho, where he committed suicide in 1961. The National Capital where Harold stood eventually became the Cuban Academy of Sciences.

Barbara May's father—my grandfather—apparently had an affinity for Cuba; re-entry documents show he also visited in the 1920s. And, sometime after Barbara May's mother died and the two sisters were on their own, their father married a woman from Cuba named Isabel. She was listed as his wife in his obituary when he died in 1965 at the age of seventy. What he liked about Cuba other than finding a wife will likely remain a mystery, although it's worth mentioning that he, like many visitors, may have simply gone there to enjoy the festive, tropical playground that was Cuba before the revolution.

In the absence of information for so many years and without the benefit of talking to my biological mother, I plowed through the letters, documents, and pictures with great intensity. Even the name Barbara became a source of fascination. It was a name I had neither liked nor disliked, but now it was a name that had personal meaning. I liked it almost instantly, not because I was drawn to the sound of the name, but because it was my mother's name.

I was equally enthralled with again exploring significant biological landmarks in and around Monmouth County. I visited Barbara May's grave for a second time, accompanied by Carol. And this time, I could without reservation call Barbara May "Mom," again tell her that I loved her, and again thank her for giving me life. More than ever, standing there at the foot of her plaque, I wished she were alive, that we could talk, that we could hold each other, that we would cry perhaps.

I also passed the two downtown Freehold buildings where Barbara May and Nancy worked after high school, Nancy as a bank bookkeeper in a building with an outside clock and Barbara as a secretary for an insurance agent in a building next door to the Carnegie Library. The charming downtown, with its red-brick sidewalks and bursts of pinks, whites, and greens flowing from flower planters, is full of history beyond my own, not the least of which is the refurbished American Hotel, circa 1924, where I stayed. President Abraham Lincoln once dropped in at the former stagecoach stop.

Nancy, Carol, Susan, and I toured from the street all the houses where Barbara May and Nancy lived during their childhood. And we stopped at the last home where Barbara May, Parker, and their children lived—a modest, two-story dwelling built by Barbara May's husband, with a red barn, several outbuildings, a small pond and vegetable garden, and a sweeping pasture where two of Barbara May's daughters, Jeanne and Lisa, rode horses. For a time, Barbara May's daughter, Diane, and son, Eddie, lived on either side of the Freehold Township property.

The new owner of the property, a New York City restaurant owner named Sal, purchased it after Barbara May and Parker died. While Carol, Nancy, and Susan waited in the car, I toured the nine-acre property with Sal and imagined the life Barbara May had there. Sal admitted he had made some changes to the property but said it still looked much like it had the day he bought it.

Inside the barn, I happened to notice an old framed lithograph featuring a rider on a muscular race horse named Blue Gown, a British thoroughbred that won the 1868 Epson Derby and Ascot Gold Cup. It is fairly obscure history, and I'm not sure what significance the horse had, if any, for Barbara May or other members of the family. Moreover, the matting and frame were not in the best shape, and it was not a particularly attractive rendering of a horse and rider. Nevertheless, I asked Sal if the lithograph had been there when he took over the property. Indeed it had, he said, and he offered it to me, sensing that I might like it because, surely, Barbara May had occasionally glanced at it or walked past it. I accepted his offer eagerly.

I had no way of safely carrying the lithograph on an airplane, so Carol agreed to have a new mat put around the image and send it to me in Indiana. I chose to keep the weathered black and gold wood frame, a passage-of-time testament, I suppose, to the time Barbara May, her husband, and their children lived there—years of family experiences I did not have the privilege of participating in.

The lithograph is now hanging on a wall in my study. It is not something I would have plunked down even five dollars for. I am not especially fond of the static, uninspiring artwork. But when I look at the nicks, scratches, and worn-away paint on the frame, I think of Barbara May and how hard she fought to thrive through adversity. I learned about some of that because while we were looking through the scrapbook, while we were riding around to see childhood homes, Barbara May's sister was talking.

In her guarded way, and at times struggling to clear the dust from memories long since buried, Nancy summoned stories of a childhood and early adulthood that seemed, for the most part, gloomy, barren, and lacking affection.

At the center of Barbara May and Nancy's childhood stood their father, largely because their mother, a caring yet strict woman, was often ill and either in bed or in the hospital. The sisters' father, meanwhile, was a complex man of vacillating moods and behaviors. He was friendly when he was drinking and less so, even angry at times, when he wasn't; sometimes Barbara May and Nancy hoped he would grab a beer or two to lighten his mood. He also suffered from several disorders—likely St. Vitas' dance and Tourette's syndrome—that made it difficult for him to climb stairs and led him to interject loud barking noises when he spoke. The latter was terribly embarrassing for Barbara May and Nancy.

The sisters were equally embarrassed by the bathing routine that existed when they were teenagers. The house they lived in at the time had running water, but no fixed bathtub. And so, every Sunday night, their father would fill a portable galvanized tub with warm water and all three children, one at a time, would bathe in the same water. When they were finished, their father would check their ears to make sure they had been cleaned. "I was fifteen years old," Nancy recalled. "You don't want your father looking at your ears at that age."

Another routine not embraced by Barbara May and Nancy stemmed from their father's worship of the sun. He frequently sunbathed, and when he couldn't go outside, he used a sun lamp. He required that the three children, goggles shielding their eyes, also use the sun lamp, sometimes daily. "I think that's why whenever I go to the dermatologist," Nancy said, "they're taking something off."

Their father also had a habit of stealthily checking up on Barbara May and Nancy, believing that the two of them were often up to no good. Sometimes, when he came home from his railroad job late at night, he would park the car down the road, walk up the driveway, and sneak into the house. Sometimes Barbara May and Nancy would hear someone approaching the house and worry there was an intruder nearby. "You're out in the country, it's midnight or whatever it was, and you hear someone walking up in the driveway," Nancy said. "You'd wonder, 'Who in the world is that?'"

The truth is, neither sister got into any significant trouble, although Nancy wasn't quite the goody-two-shoes she claims she was. She once ran away from home to Anastasia's house, something she doesn't recall Barbara May ever doing. Barbara May, meanwhile, had "a mouth on her," often defied authority, and "was outspoken in an age when women didn't do that sort of thing." And both sisters participated in childhood capers that would elicit only mild rebukes from parents today. They stole flowers from a neighbor's garden so they could sell them and buy ice cream with the proceeds, and they once lined a mattress with newspapers in the bed of a relative they didn't like.

Perhaps it was the relatively slim pickings at home that led to the flower caper. There was always food to eat, but it was usually food from the vegetable garden, like lima beans and tomatoes. Every now and then, the children would have what were considered delicacies: canned peaches, tuna fish, or chicken noodle soup.

The furnishings in their childhood homes were similarly scant. One home's room in particular was completely bare except for an old Victrola smack-dab in the middle of the room. Barbara May, Nancy, and Howard would put old records on the Victrola and march around it. That is a rare fond memory for Nancy.

When the children's mother died, Nancy recalled thinking, "I can't believe this is happening." But she then went about the business of moving on, because that's what one did in those days. "I remember my brother coming up to me at the funeral home and looking in the casket and saying to me, 'Why is Mommy laying there so quiet?' I don't remember how I answered him."

Nancy similarly accepted without angst the paucity of affection in the Shinn household. "People in our family cared about each other, but they weren't overly affectionate. For me, I just accepted it the way it was."

Still, the lack of demonstrable love likely had consequences in Nancy's adult life.

"I'm not a very social person," said Nancy, who has lived alone since her husband died in 2001. "I have to know somebody first. And the word love is very difficult for me. I don't know if it was difficult for my sister. I can show love for a baby. I can show love for an animal. I can show love for my girls. But when it's an adult, I don't know what it is. It's very hard for me to say it. It's a very complex word."

In truth, the general absence of affection or encouragement may have affected Barbara May even more than her sister. Nancy recalled that because Barbara May wasn't the best student, some teachers would say to her, "I don't know what I'm going to do with you. Why can't you be like your sister?" That must have sliced into Barbara May's self-esteem.

Closer to home, a relative once told Barbara May that her father hadn't wanted her because he wanted a boy. Then, after her mother's health declined precipitously after giving birth to Howard, Barbara May was blamed by her father for her mother's ill health because it had taken another pregnancy to produce a boy, relatives said. That would have been a wound not easily healed.

There was also the matter of Barbara May's strained relationship with Nancy, which was made worse, Nancy said, when their mother died and Nancy tried to become the mother figure. "I didn't realize the resentment then," Nancy said, "but I learned about it in later years."

There were so many differences between the two sisters. Barbara May was the extrovert and Nancy was the introvert. Barbara May found ways to visit friends and Nancy stayed mostly at home. Barbara May sometimes seemed older than her years and Nancy was, at best, naïve.

Nancy said the two sisters rarely did things together, but one vivid memory stood out: the time Barbara May taught her about the birds and the bees. Nancy was sixteen and Barbara May was fourteen.

"How she knew about that stuff, I don't know," Nancy said.

The sisters had just finished watching the 1946 movie *To Each His Own* starring Olivia de Havilland, and they were walking down Havens Bridge Road in Howell Township, New Jersey. In the film, de Havilland's character, Jody, has an intense, one-night fling with a World War I pilot named Bart. ("There's some sort of crazy magic between you and me," he tells her.) The fling leads to a pregnancy and Jody gives birth to a son out of wedlock after Bart's death in the war. Through a series of painful events, the child winds up with another woman. Jody has to love her son from afar—until she reunites with him at his wedding and mother and son share a dance.

"I don't know if I was naïve or just not with it," Nancy said, "but Barbara was the one who taught me the facts of life on that walk home from the movie. She told me how babies were made and I was so taken aback I just didn't want to talk about it. I don't remember the exact words she used. I just remember that she knew more than I did."

Six years later, Barbara May, like the character in the movie, also faced the prospect of giving up her child, although the circumstances were quite different. As she had done with her daughter, Carol, Nancy shared with me the vague details of the train trip Barbara May, Nancy, and Anastasia took to Tarrytown, New York, so Barbara May could give birth to me. She added this twist: she believes Anastasia also thought the father was Barbara May's future husband, Parker Bohn, who was married to another woman at the time; Nancy remembers Anastasia remarking, "Let's hope what she's going through will make her realize that relationship has to end."

Anastasia died in 1987 at the age of eighty-three, so we may never know if she asked who the father of the child was or talked with Barbara May about responsible behavior.

Nancy, though, seemed to understand how Barbara May wound up in such a predicament, given the sisters' challenging childhoods.

Barbara May, she said, "was just a young girl looking for love."

Chapter Fourteen

Almost from the beginning, Barbara May's daughter, Diane, called me brother. Not half-brother. Brother. She said it matter-of-factly with a disarming sweetness: "You're my brother."

I met Diane and her husband one month after meeting Carol and Nancy in New Jersey. We chose a hotel just north of Louisville, Kentucky, about halfway between my condo in Fort Wayne and Diane's rural home seventy-five miles outside of Nashville, Tennessee.

I arrived first, and fifteen minutes later watched Diane check in at the front desk, all six foot one of her. Height, I would come to learn, runs in my biological mother's side of the family. Relatives said Barbara May's other son, Eddie, is six foot four, Lisa is six foot two, and Jeanne is about five foot eight. Barbara May was five ten. I'm six foot three, maybe closer to six two now, having shrunk with age.

I recognized Diane immediately, not because I had seen any recent photographs of her or because we look alike; we are neither profoundly similar nor dissimilar. I recognized her because whatever bond we had forged over the phone or in emails followed us into that hotel, drawing us together through the invisible forces I acknowledge but will never understand.

I had checked in and put my belongings in my first-floor room. Periodically, I would poke my head out and look down the hallway toward the front counter in the lobby. When Diane arrived, I began walking toward her and she must have sensed my presence because she turned toward me. In that moment, I could tell she knew who I was too.

"Diane?" I said.

"Rick?"

"Good to see you," I said.

And then we hugged, tightly. I felt a catch in my throat, tears rising, and I think she cried a little too.

Nine hours later, our bond would be even stronger—through laughter, tears, and more hugs, long and firm.

We sat in my hotel room, two siblings now in their sixties, and talked, looked over documents and pictures, and marveled at a story decades in the making that had fallen in our laps. I couldn't stop thinking, "That's my sister." I couldn't stop looking at her eyes, her nose, her lips, her blonde hair, her hands, her long legs, her gentle, cherubic smile; looking for similar physical features, and there were a few. I wondered if she was looking at me the same way.

Among the items Diane brought with her was our mother's Freehold High School yearbook, "The Log," which included below each senior's headshot a nickname, a quote, and a list of school activities the student had participated in. Barbara May's read:

BARBARA SHINN
Bobbie
"Come live, and be merry, and join with me."
Hallowe'en Painting 4; Committees: Prom, Yearbook; Clubs: Dancing 1, 2, 4.

Bobbie apparently was not a nickname that stayed with our mother later in life. The quote, meanwhile, was a mystery eventually solved: It is a passage in a poem called "Laughing Song" by English poet and painter William Blake, first printed in 1789 in a collection entitled "Songs of Innocence." Barbara May was likely not a connoisseur of such literature, and so perhaps her high school had compiled a list of quotes from which students could choose.

Barbara May's yearbook was also filled with affectionate inscriptions from fellow students, including many from young men. A boy named Smitty wrote, "Barb, To a swell girl. The best of everything." A football player named Alton and nicknamed Chico wrote, "Dear Bobby, With your charm & figure, I'm sure you will go far." He must have been rather charming himself. Then there was Gil, who wrote, "Lots of luck and happiness" before crossing out "happiness" and replacing it with "success." "Don't forget," he added, "to name the first one after me. Gil" Clearly our mother did not take that to heart.

Gil's family said he was something of a jokester in high school and was merely pulling Barbara May's leg. The two had apparently known each other since elementary school.

Gil went on to get a bachelor's degree in mechanical engineering and later earned a law degree, although he never practiced law. He became a patent examiner for the U.S. Patent and Trademark Office, and for a long time was the mayor of an east coast town, according to one of his two daughters. By 2018, he and his wife, also a Freehold High School graduate, had been married for sixty-five years.

I could have lived with the name Gil, I suppose, if for no other reason than two fine baseball players of yesteryear had that name—Gil Hodges and Gil McDougald. Hodges was a native of Indiana, where I now live. McDougald died in Wall Township, New Jersey, where Barbara May spent many years watching car racing.

Diane also brought our mother's senior-year grades transcript, and the scholastic problems Barbara May exhibited in the earlier grades had obviously persisted. Our mother just wasn't a very good student. She did get an *A* in Stenography and a *B* in Art, but it went downhill from there, including *D*s in U.S. History and, of all things, English.

I can't profess that I ever became a good student, and in that arena we had a lot in common. But when it came to English, the apple apparently fell a fair distance from the tree.

Diane and I had a good laugh about that. But periodically, there were tears as she sat looking at me. The tears came from a place deep inside her because she had considered our mother her best friend, someone who would have told her anything. And yet, there was one thing Barbara May hadn't told her, and for Diane that triggered a pain that was raw then and still with her when she and I visited again nine months later in Nashville. Thinking about the anguish Barbara May went through leading up to my birth and the secret she kept every year thereafter was simply overwhelming for Diane, who to this day keeps a picture of our mother in her SUV.

"I wish Mom had told me," she said. "If she was alive, I would have gone to her and said the name Richard Alan Shinn. And I would have said, 'Mom, he's found us. We need to see him.' And that's what we would have done.

"I know that every morning when she woke up she thought of you. I know that every day she loved you. I'd like to think that she has a smile on her face now, now that we've met."

Diane is certain about a few other things, too: Our mother did, she believes, give Eddie the middle name of Richard in memory of me, and Barbara May would have delighted in meeting me, would have welcomed me with open arms. Loving, after all, was in her nature.

"She was caring, she was loving, she was kind, she didn't have a mean bone in her body," Diane said. "Mom was my best friend and anything that bothered me in school, I told her."

Part of Barbara May's loving was making sure her children were accountable for their actions. Diane recounted one incident when, at the age of eighteen, she got drunk on screwdrivers and Long Island iced teas at a benefit for a local race car driver who had died.

"She read me the riot act," Diane said, "and told me, 'You better not let your father see you like this.'" The reason: Barbara May's husband, Parker, was against drinking alcohol, stemming from his experience with a father who was a drinker.

So that night, Barbara May clandestinely drove Diane home, where Diane promptly threw up and went to bed. At five the next morning, Barbara May roused Diane from her sleep and told her: "If you think you're old enough to drink, you're old enough to get up and help me with chores."

Diane recalled that Barbara May somehow made life good in a blended family that included her four children and four children from Parker's previous marriage. Parker's children were not at all happy to be thrust into a new family after their father left his first wife and married Barbara May in 1955. Diane said they blamed Barbara May for their parents' divorce.

After Barbara May died, Diane looked over Barbara May's checkbooks and discovered that our mother and Parker had basically lived paycheck to paycheck, although the children never noticed. The family seemed to have everything they needed on Parker's earnings as a dock builder. If there was any financial stress, Barbara May and Parker kept it hidden.

Diane recalled milking cows on the family spread in Freehold Township and drinking the warm milk unpasteurized. "I tell people I'm still here, so it didn't hurt me." The family also ate produce from the garden—tomatoes, peppers, watermelon, cantaloupes, eggplants, carrots, and string beans—and raised chickens and goats.

Diane and Eddie rode dirt bikes on the property, Jeanne and Lisa showed the horses, and all of the children except Diane took up car racing to greater or lesser degrees. A favorite memory, Diane said, was hooking up a sleigh to a black horse named Shadow and riding through the snow in winter, jingle bells and all.

Barbara May always seemed happy, especially at Wall Stadium on race nights, and especially when she listened to Elvis, not Nat King Cole, as it turns out. Even when health issues began emerging at about the age of forty-nine, Barbara May gravitated to good cheer. She survived colon cancer surgery and chemotherapy, then a short time later liver cancer surgery. In her later years, she survived a mild stroke and heart attack, and also struggled with high blood pressure. Finally, it was the aortic aneurysm—the same condition I had—that proved too much to overcome. That she lived to seventy-three was something of a miracle. Her brother, Howard, was not so fortunate. He died of colon cancer in 1992 in Arizona at the age of fifty-four.

I can't say for certain that I would have managed my lifestyle better if I'd known my biological family's medical history. Maybe I would have eaten better. Maybe, like Barbara May, Nancy, and their mother, I wouldn't have taken up smoking. Maybe I would have managed my stress more effectively.

But while I can't start over, I have begun taking better care of myself in the hopes I can buy a few more productive years. And my cardiologist has been carefully monitoring me since the age of forty-five, when I had the first of two heart attacks.

The first hit on a Monday. I woke up feeling crummy and thought I might be on the verge of a panic attack. I told my wife I intended to take the day off from work, then spent the next six or so hours curled in a fetal position in bed, ignoring what I later learned are signature warning signs of a heart attack: pain in the jaw and left arm, periodic sweating, and tightness in the chest. At 2 P.M., I called my wife at work and told her I wanted to knock whatever it was out of my system by hitting golf balls at the driving range with her when she got off work. And that's exactly what we did. I hit at least fifty golf balls, took a break, realized I could barely breathe, and on the walk back to the car stopped to sit down three times. My wife insisted on taking me to the emergency room, and I consented, but only if I walked in under my own power. No wheelchairs. No stretchers. No guiding arms. It's crazy, I know, but I've always believed that if I'm upright, I can beat anything. And if by some chance I get knocked down, it is imperative that I get back up as quickly as possible. It's that warrior spirit thing again—an ingrained belief that I must fight for everything. For acceptance. For recognition. For survival.

So, when we got to the hospital, I walked in without assistance, told the woman at the front desk that I didn't feel well and, minimizing my discomfort, said that I might be having a panic attack. That landed me at the bottom of the list of patients waiting to be examined, and it was a good forty-five minutes before an intuitive doctor ordered an EKG. A short time after that, the curtains to my room flew open and an army of medical professionals rushed in, hooked me up to all manner of lines and tubes, and ran morphine through my IV.

"Mr. Farrant," a doctor said, "you are having a heart attack."

"Right now?"

"Yes, right now."

I likely had been suffering a heart attack for most of the day; fortunately my inaction had only left a small piece of my heart damaged. Later, a surgeon inserted two stents to open a clogged artery, and I experienced no lasting ill effects.

When the second heart attack hit at the age of fifty-eight, I was much more attentive and responsive. I identified the symptoms quickly, had my wife drive me to the hospital, again walked in on my own, and told the woman at the front desk, "I have had a heart attack before and I think I'm having one now." There was no delay in the hospital response this time and I eventually had another four stents placed in an artery.

Since the first heart attack, I have been on medicines to lower my cholesterol, thin my blood, and keep my blood pressure in check. I have also been dutiful about getting periodic colonoscopies, I exercise regularly, and I am working on my diet.

Even though learning about my genetic predisposition for heart attacks and cancer came too late in life for any longer-term preventive measures, it did provide at least one interesting twist. For years, doctors and nurses would ask me if I had any particular malady or condition that ran in my family. "I don't know," I would say. "I am adopted." And the doctors and nurses would nod, as if that's all the explaining that needed to be done. Today, I can recite chapter and verse the health problems that have beset my biological relatives.

Those conditions are one of Barbara May's legacies, but so, too, is her gentle, loving, hopeful heart, now mirrored in Diane's character. It's as if I can see my biological mother through her. I felt this one Sunday in early September 2018 during my second visit with Diane in Nashville. We were no longer strangers, easily slipping into good-natured brother-sister teasing, but also into genuine expressions of love. At one point, Diane hooked her arm in mine. At another, we held hands as we walked through the lush gardens of the Gaylord Opryland Hotel.

Just as I had no playbook for what it meant to be a good man, particularly in the context of a marriage, I have no guide, as an only child, for what it means to be a good brother. All I know is that I love the feeling of sibling interaction and affection. I love the idea that I have brothers and sisters, even if I never meet all of them. Even if a few of them never decide to accept me.

Eddie is one who *has* embraced me. When he learned through Sal that I had visited the old homestead, he sent me a text inviting me to call him. "Sounds like you are my half-brother I did not know I had. Great news!"

He later sent me a photo of him and his son posing with racing legend Mario Andretti. Both father and son, now living in North Carolina, are still involved in the racing business.

In a subsequent phone call, Eddie told me more about the NASCAR circuit than I ever could have imagined knowing. And in 2019, we met for lunch in Charlotte while I was visiting my daughter. The conversation was pleasant and not at all awkward. It was as if we had known each other for years.

I told him I hoped he would one day arrange for me to sit in a race car—perhaps even drive one. That would be befitting of a Shinn.

Chapter Fifteen

I never felt the urge to find my biological father. I think that had something to do with the intrinsic bond between mother and child; that the child is, upon arrival, closest to the mother, if for no other reason than she carried the child in her womb. Even when I didn't know who my birth mother was, I felt we were a part of each other. My biological father, meanwhile, was at best a contributor to my existence and, based on the adoption agency narrative, not even around at the time of my birth.

Nevertheless, as I moved ever near to confirming the relationship between Barbara May and me, I noticed close relatives listed in ancestry.com who didn't seem to have any link to the Shinn genealogy. One woman in particular, Lilly, appeared to be a half-sibling; her centimorgan count in relation to me was 1,767. Another woman, Rhonda, had a centimorgan count of 999 and appeared to be a first cousin.

I reached out to both women via the ancestry website and told them about my adoption, my growing conviction that Barbara May was my mother, and that my biological roots were in Monmouth County, New Jersey. I also mentioned all of the tangential names associated with the Shinn family. Rhonda didn't respond, but Lilly did and wrote this:

Rick,

I do not recognize any of the names you mentioned—not even one. However, Monmouth County rings a loud bell because parts of my family (Slocum) go back there to the 1660s! I was born there in 1948.

Perhaps by tracing some of the names you have you can find a Slocum connection?

Lilly

Lilly, who was born a Slocum but now goes by her married name, never corresponded again. Perhaps she grew fearful when I began piecing information together that indicated the Slocum name might indeed be the key to my paternal origin, and that it looked like her father might be my father. That man was James Russell Slocum Sr., who died in 1996 at the age of sixty-seven.

I learned through online documents that he had been in the heating and cooling business and, as a member of the Wall Township Fire Department, named Fireman of the Year in 1981. He and his wife had raised two sons and three daughters. He had two brothers: one deceased and one in his nineties still living in 2017. The deceased brother was Rhonda's father.

I discovered another of James' daughters on Facebook—Barbara—and began a slow dance of genealogical discovery with her. As with many other newfound relatives, she was suspicious and hesitant at first, but gradually began to accept the unthinkable: that her father, who seemed to have had a picture-perfect, nearly fifty-year marriage to his wife and was a terrific father to his children, might have had an affair with Barbara May when he was twenty-three with two young children at home.

That thought was uncomfortable for me, too, because my intent was never to upend a family, even if it meant getting at the truth of my lineage. It would be hard for any family, especially one so rooted in a secure history, to fathom such a dark secret.

But Barbara pushed on. She sent me pictures of her father and of other family members, I sent her pictures of me, and we engaged in a long-running exercise of trying to determine physical similarities. A few photos of her father somewhat resembled me at various times in my life, and her older brother, Tommy, looked a lot like me when we were both younger.

The adoption agency's description of my father, which stemmed from information my biological mother had provided, was initially confusing based on my discussions with Barbara. The depiction that he was 5'11" and weighing 170 pounds with curly brown hair and brown eyes sounded about right to Barbara. But he was not "in the Army at the time" of my conception, and in fact had never been in the Army. He had served a short stint in the Navy when he was younger.

I speculated that perhaps Barbara May had either made that part up in an attempt to protect him or had misunderstood the timing and nature of his military service. But it was enough of a contradiction that I convinced Barbara to submit her DNA to ancestry.com. My thinking was that the results would confirm she was Lilly's sister and that, coupled with Barbara's centimorgan count in relation to me, would confirm her as my half-sibling and prove that James Russell Slocum Sr. was my father.

Here, though, is where DNA results and analyses sometime get tricky. Barbara's centimorgan count clearly linked her as a sister to Lilly, but the count in relation to me was 1,470—at the low end of the half-sibling range. While the vast majority of the other factors seemed to point to her being my half-sibling and James Russell Slocum Sr. being my father, the centimorgan revelation seemed inconclusive enough to warrant further examination. I suggested to Barbara that she and I download all of our raw ancestry.com DNA data to gedmatch.com, an open source DNA database that provides more in-depth genetic analysis tools. They are the same tools that law enforcement professionals have begun using with great success—and some controversy—to track down criminals.

To help me decipher the gedmatch results, I sought assistance from genealogical researcher Karin Corbeil, co-founder, director, and executive vice president of dnaadoption.org, a non-profit that aims to teach and guide people searching for their biological roots. Karin and others like her at dnaadoption.org are referred to as "search angels."

For the novice, trying to read the results of gedmatch.com pairings is akin to trying to learn a foreign language. It is complicated stuff, especially the twenty-three colorful chromosome bars. But Karin, working with another gedmatch volunteer, came to an unequivocal conclusion that Karin first shared with me and then with Barbara in this highly technical March 3, 2018 email:

Barbara,

There is no doubt in my mind that you and Lilly are half sisters to Rick.

The amount of DNA you share is absolutely within the range of half siblings. Half siblings will fall into a range of about 1,320-2,100 cMs (centimorgans). This range is confirmed by other proven half sibling relationships. Also, the fact that you do not share anything on the X chromosome tells us that this is a paternal match (males only receive their X chromosome from their mothers).

Other relationships that might fall into the range of your match with Rick would be grandparent/grandchild, aunt/nephew/uncle/niece or double 1st cousins. You and Rick do not share any FIRs (Fully Identical Regions) on your matching segments, so we can eliminate double 1st cousins. And obviously, grandparent/grandchild is not what we are seeing. An aunt/nephew or uncle/niece can also be eliminated because half siblings should have fewer but longer segments than an aunt/nephew. This is the case with you and Rick.

The reason you have 1,470 cMs and Lilly has 1,767 cMs with Rick is only due to the randomness of DNA being passed down from your parents. Lilly obviously received just a little more from your father but you are both within the confirmed range of half siblings to Rick.

I hope this answers your questions and if you have any others, please feel free to write me. I have totally enjoyed working with Rick and appreciate the help you have given him. I truly hope that any conflicts with your siblings get resolved. I'm sure they will once they may agree and meet Rick!

I wish you all well.

Best regards,
Karin Corbeil

Karin's centimorgan range for half-siblings was a bit more liberal than ancestry.com's (1,400-2,050), but that did not change the conclusion. Barbara was officially my half-sister and James Russell Slocum Sr. was my father. Barbara's older brother, Tommy, would later submit his DNA to ancestry.com and his results (1,907 centimorgans) confirmed he was my half-brother.

Not only had I found my biological father—something I never had imagined—I now had nine half-brothers and sisters. But like some of the siblings on my mother's side, some of my father's children were equally resistant to know me or dubious about the science.

Karin's mention of conflict with siblings was a reference to Lilly's abrupt halt in correspondence with me and apparent disinterest in discussing the matter with other family members, as well as Tommy's initial reluctance to accept the facts. I could have added half-sister Jeanne's inexplicable and abrupt decision to stop corresponding with me after initially being so helpful in my search for my mother.

Access to public DNA databases has brought some wonderful opportunities for discovery, but it has also exposed secrets that can shock and divide families, not to mention make vulnerable to rejection those seeking biological connections. Karin has had a front-row seat to people's stories and personally understands the frustration of looking for biological family members without DNA assistance. She was adopted through the same New York agency Barbara May worked with after I was born, and spent thirty years looking for her mother and father.

Like me, she discovered her birth name through adoption papers, placed her birth name with the ALMA Society, and conducted numerous online searches using the birth name. Like me, she received non-identifying information from Spence-Chapman. Like me, she wasn't looking for a replacement family, although her childhood with her adopted family was decidedly better than mine.

"I had an awesome life with my adoptive parents," she said. "Some people don't have that, and they're looking for the fairytale."

Karin ran into numerous dead ends in her search, but by examining U.S. Census data, she eventually pieced together information that led to her mother's family. She learned her mother and father had married about a year after she was born. Her mother had died at thirty-two, a brother at twenty-nine, and her father at fifty-six. She developed a good relationship with a surviving brother.

All of this she accomplished without the benefit of public DNA databases, but her struggles inspired her to help develop the scientific methodology that would assist others. One thing the Brooklyn, New York native will tell you, though, is this: don't count on a fairytale ending.

Karin said an estimated 30 percent of people using DNA search methods are hit with a surprise, and sometimes that surprise is unpleasant, such as learning someone's purported father is not their father. Or in the case of my adopted daughter Amber—who was told by biological family members she had Native American ancestry—learning that not a smidgeon of Native American ethnicity turned up in her ancestry.com DNA analysis.

"I'm seeing surprises more and more, because more people are testing," Karin said. "You tell people, 'Hey, there could be a surprise. You need to be aware of that.'"

The other caveat, Karin said, is that newfound family members aren't always welcoming. There is a fair amount of rejection going on.

Upbeat commercials for ancestry.com and similar sites don't come with warning labels mentioning the possibility of painful outcomes. They don't say that secrets some people thought they would take to their graves will no longer be secrets, or that some relatives will be less than pleased.

My experience, though, has been that the acceptances have mostly outweighed the rejections, and that some of the surprises, even some of the lingering mysteries, have been so fascinating that they have largely mitigated any pain.

Here is one of the surprises, and it's similar to learning that my biological mother may have given the middle name of Richard to son Eddie in remembrance of me. According to my half-sister Barbara, our biological father was the one who named her Barbara and she believes it's possible it may have been in remembrance of Barbara May. No one could have suspected that before I came along, because no one in the Slocum family knew about me.

Over the course of phone calls and Facebook messages, Barbara helped fill in other pieces about her father's life. Barbara was James Russell Slocum Sr.'s second youngest child and grew up in New Jersey with an older brother and younger sister. The two oldest children, Lilly and Tommy, had grown up and left home.

Her father—my father—was born on Oct. 6, 1928 in Belmar, New Jersey, in Monmouth County. According to Barbara and military records, James Sr. dropped out of Manasquan High School in 1945 at the age of seventeen to join the Navy. He met his future wife on April 1, 1946—April Fool's Day—when he walked into Francis Sweet Shop on Main Street in Bradley Beach, New Jersey. His future wife, then a high school student, was working at the sweet shop serving lavish banana splits and sundaes, and James Sr. was instantly taken with her. He later told one of his relatives, "Today I met the girl I'm going to marry." The two married on June 21, 1947 and stayed together until James died from cancer on March 31, 1996 in West Palm Beach, Florida. His wife died in Lake Worth, Florida, on Oct. 15, 2015 at the age of eighty-six.

James Sr. never finished high school—another baffling contradiction of the adoption agency's account. In addition to being a volunteer firefighter in Wall, N.J., and holding down a series of jobs throughout his life, he coached Little League baseball and loved country music.

Barbara recalls an idyllic childhood and said her parents had a loving and what seemed like made-in-heaven marriage. The children saw them kiss and hold hands often, and a friend once told Barbara it was undeniably obvious that they were in love.

The Slocums, with the three younger children in tow, made numerous trips to Miami Beach, where they always stayed in the same motel (The Duane on 83rd Street) and always stayed in the same room. Like Barbara May's father, James Sr. loved the sun. Every day, the family would walk to the beach. Every night, they would go to dinner. James Sr. and his wife eventually moved to West Palm Beach in 1986.

Barbara said her father made Christmases magical, singing along with all the seasonal songs, and he loved to tell stories about his childhood, including tales of getting into trouble. Again, it was the kind of trouble that pales in comparison to today's juvenile delinquencies.

In one story, he and a friend climbed a water tower in West Belmar, New Jersey. In another, he and his brothers got into trouble for smoking. James Sr. had taken up smoking at the age of nine and smoked until the day he died.

"He loved telling old stories," Barbara said. "I didn't care if I heard them a hundred times, I never got tired of hearing them."

Like Barbara May, he had a nickname when he was younger: Sparky. He acquired the name when he experienced a severe electrical shock while doing his heating and cooling work. Perhaps Barbara May knew him as Sparky and he knew Barbara May as Bobbie. Perhaps it was just Jim and Barb or James and Barbara, or perhaps they had their own nicknames for each other.

My half-sister Barbara, a nanny who now lives in Georgia with her husband, is a person of faith and compassion who for a considerable time did not want to believe that her beloved father had strayed while married. But as science increasingly collided with certainty, she landed on two very simple thoughts that helped her cope with the shocking reality. "Stuff happens" was one of them. The other was conjecture that maybe her father was reeling under the weight of a young marriage with two young kids at home and that he found relief in the arms of another woman—my biological mother.

Neither Barbara nor I will ever know what prompted him to strike up a relationship with my mother. And it's unlikely he ever told his wife about her, especially given that he apparently named a daughter Barbara.

But if he did name one of his children in memory of my biological mother, it would suggest that his feelings for her were more than a passing interest.

Chapter Sixteen

My half-sisters Diane and Barbara are adamant about two things. Diane says Barbara May never would have told my father about me. She wouldn't have wanted to upend his family life. Barbara, meanwhile, believes her father would have, in some fashion, taken responsibility for getting Barbara May pregnant had he known.

So, in all likelihood, my father never knew about me, and it's plausible that he never told anyone about his relationship with Barbara May. My mother, on the other hand, may have told someone, because Diane recalls hearing once that she and her siblings might have a half-brother somewhere. She can't recall where she heard it, but the information didn't come from Barbara May or sister Nancy.

It's also possible that Barbara May had a relationship with more than one man and that she didn't know who the father of her baby was. That could explain the discrepancies in the description of my father Barbara May gave to the adoption agency. I choose to discount that theory simply because I want to think well of my biological mother. That is, admittedly, hypocritical of me given my relationship track record, which at times bordered on promiscuous. But for me, intimate encounters were always more about acceptance than conquest. They were about equating my partner's sexual willingness with love. To be fair to Barbara May, she may have pursued sexual relationships for the same reasons I did—to feel wanted, valued, and to patch the emotional wounds of a difficult childhood.

In any event, I have the freedom to build the imaginative narrative of how my biological mother and father consummated their relationship—something no one likely knows six decades after my birth, and certainly something the wonderful science of genetics can't provide.

The two young lovers might have met at Wall Stadium. One of my father's sons, Tommy, recalls that his father and uncles spent a lot of time there and took Tommy when he was young. Or perhaps my biological mother and father met at a nearby roller rink in Wall, since they both enjoyed roller skating. It's also possible they met by chance at a mutual friend's house or at one of several community activities, such as a dance or a movie, then got to know each other over burgers, fries, and shakes at a stainless-steel-wrapped New Jersey diner. Or perhaps my father had business at the Freehold insurance agency where Barbara May worked and one thing led to another.

Several blunt friends of mine have suggested a cruder story line: Barbara May and my father may have unceremoniously hooked up somewhere and had a one-night stand, experiencing a fleeting—and costly—paradise by the dashboard light, apologies to Meat Loaf. I can live with that story too, but again, I'd rather not. And this time, the reason is more about my worth than judging Barbara May if she did indeed have a one-night fling. I'd like to think there was some measure of love that led to my existence, which would make me, at least from my perspective, less of a mistake. No one, I don't think, likes to think of themselves as a mistake. The thought of being the result of an incidental slipup has been disquieting at times.

I did try to uncover the origin of my mother and father's relationship. I spent hours on the internet over several days looking at hundreds of 1950s-era pictures of Wall Stadium, New Jersey roller rinks, diners and dances, and other social activities. I scrutinized scenes of Monmouth County locales, including photos of Union Beach, where as a young child I waded in water near my adopted grandmother's summer home, just fifteen miles or so from Freehold—and from Barbara May and James.

The internet search was fascinating, but as I expected, I found not a single picture that resembled Barbara May or James. That left me with my imagination. It is the same imagination that concocted the ridiculous notion that my biological mother followed me around the country throughout my life.

In the end, I suppose it doesn't really matter how I was conceived, only that Barbara May gave me life. But I will always harken back to the early 1950s and wonder. I am simply drawn by a yearning to visualize how my biological mother and father met and loved.

. . .

In my flights of fancy, spinning a yarn mostly fictional save for some geographical and historical details, I see two well-meaning people of occasionally compromised consciences, Barbara May searching for affection and worried that her obsession with Parker, her eventual husband, will lead to nothing, and James looking for a breath of freedom to lighten the load of a young marriage, two young children, and all of the responsibilities that come with a growing family.

I see Barbara May and James in the chilly early Friday evening of February 29, 1952 arriving separately at a roller rink in Wall to shake off a challenging work week and loosen the tethers of adulthood. Barbara May is dressed in a knee-high skirt, cardigan, and wears her hair carefully coiffed; James wears jeans, a flannel shirt, and his curly hair is prematurely receding. They meet as they each take a break in rented skates at the edge of the sleek hardwood floor. The conversation is halting at first, but gradually Barbara May and James feel the tug of infatuation—or something—and they agree to meet again for lunch the following afternoon. Barbara May gives James a quick, warm peck on the neck and James looks around to make sure no one has seen it. He is, after all, married.

The next day dawns with a dusting of snow and temperatures just below freezing. Barbara May and James arrive at a gleaming Silk City Diner in Wall that would many years later be featured on a Bon Jovi album cover, in a Springsteen video, and in the first-love romance *Baby It's You*, starring Rosanna Arquette and Vincent Spano. In a red-cushioned booth, Barbara May on one side, James on the other, their knees touch, then their shoes, then one of them reaches out to hold the hand of the other. And in that moment, their eyes lock, their hearts race, their most primordial spirits soar, and they are at once lost in a bubble of hormonal bliss.

Barbara May and James begin rambling. About their childhoods. Their likes and dislikes. About James' short stint in the Navy. About things they might do together when the weather warms, like catch a movie at the Fly-In Drive-In Theatre in Wall or spend a day visiting Asbury Park. And then out of the blue, James, feeling suddenly guilty and awkward, tells Barbara May he's married. Tells her it will be hard to find activities that don't run the risk of being found out. Barbara May isn't surprised by the revelation, even though James is not wearing his wedding ring. Barbara May had sensed James was married, because somewhere in her exists an attraction to married men. They seem to her more mature, more settled; she is naturally pulled toward a life she wants but hasn't yet achieved. Even if it's someone else's life.

Barbara May suggests that they go to her apartment to continue their conversation shielded from prying eyes and ears, and in that cocoon of safety Barbara May and James lovingly consummate their relationship. Afterwards, in the dim light of a bedroom with curtains drawn, they lie together, side by side, and wonder silently what could have been were it not for one inescapable obstacle.

In the days that follow, Barbara May and James are consumed with the emptiness that accompanies a union fated to end, and Barbara May is not surprised when James drops by her apartment and lets her know he can't continue, that he is compelled to renew his commitment to his family. Barbara May tells him she understands and the two hug and kiss briefly. It is the last time they will be together, although through the years they will occasionally see each other from afar in the stands at Wall Stadium and feel a twinge of loss.

When Barbara May realizes she is pregnant, she goes to the place that has always been a sanctuary—Aunt Anastasia's home in Toms River—and her aunt tells her in kind terms that she must go away for a while. Pregnancies out of wedlock are scandalous in the 1950s, and it is essential that women who don't choose dangerous and illegal abortions disappear to save them and their family from the embarrassing mark of promiscuity. Anastasia doesn't ask questions but tells Barbara May she'll find a good home for unwed mothers and make the arrangements. Barbara May eventually leaves Monmouth County for the home in Tarrytown, New York, when she can no longer hide the child that is growing inside of her.

There are plenty of opportunities for distraction in the spring, summer and fall of 1952. The M&M stars are sensations everywhere they go. Mickey Mantle, like Barbara May just 20 years old, is playing in his first full season with the New York Yankees and will finish with 23 home runs and a .311 batting average. Marilyn Monroe, meanwhile, is suddenly a major film star and sex symbol described by one gossip columnist as the "it girl" of 1952. In one of her many public appearances, she tours an orphanage in New Jersey—an emotional visit for her because as a child, she spent time in an orphanage and in numerous foster homes. She never knew who her biological father was.

The year also sees one of the greatest films of all time—*Singin' in the Rain* starring Gene Kelly, Debbie Reynolds, and Donald O'Connor—premiere at Radio City Music Hall. The "Jackie Gleason Show" debuts on CBS. And the iconic Mr. Potato Head toy is introduced with great fanfare.

Little of this, if any, registers with Barbara May. She is largely alone with her thoughts and reflections and feeling very much an outcast. One question consumes her: should she keep the child or put it up for adoption? In the years after the 1938 *LIFE* magazine article about St. Faith's House, homes for unwed mothers, adoption agencies, and the families of unwed mothers increasingly supported adoption over keeping a child. That pressure, along with the uncertain future of raising a child as a single woman, clashes head-on with Barbara May's desire to have children. Eleven of them, she said once, when she was much younger.

On December 4, 1952, when she gives birth to a baby boy in a Yonkers hospital, she is still conflicted. She has loved him for nine months and now that he has arrived, she holds him closely to her chest. She kisses his forehead, counts his fingers and toes, and runs her hands across his arms and legs. She smiles and sobs, sometimes simultaneously. In the moments in between, when her emotions plateau, she wishes that she and Richard Alan Shinn could go home together and somehow make do. That would be the easiest decision emotionally. But Barbara May has, by necessity, grown up some. She cannot realistically envision a prosperous life with a baby in tow. In the end, she makes the hard choice.

• • •

There are probably hundreds of other comforting versions I could concoct about the joining of Barbara May and James and the aftermath of that experience. I won't spend the rest of my life creating them. On that score, I haven't even the faintest expectation that I will ever know the true story.

My fervent hope is simply that Barbara May and James did have a "warm, caring relationship," as the adoption agency suggested. No matter how brief that relationship might have been.

Chapter Seventeen

When I wasn't playing baseball, I spent summers during my high school years in Pound Ridge fishing the streams, ponds and lakes that seemed to intersect everywhere above ground or below it.

Usually, I would fish alone, sometimes for hours at time. I found unparalleled tranquility at the water's edge casting spinners, poppers, and night crawlers, waiting for strikes. Rarely did I go home empty-handed.

Fishing was at the core of my early development—in the pre-dawn during a summer camp in Augusta, Maine when, at the age of twelve, several campmates and I walked to a nearby lake and cast for whitefish and pickerel as a milky morning mist spread across the water; when J.C. and I spent several weeks at his father's cabin in upstate New York and a summer in and around Baxter State Park in Maine, exploring waterways in a wooden Old Town canoe and eating wild berries and the few fish we caught; and when I accompanied two friends and their parents on an outing in Long Island Sound, where I caught a four-foot sand tiger shark while fishing for flounder.

Most of the fishing, though, occurred closer to home, and one teenage fishing excursion was especially memorable. J.C. and I decided to try a different route to a Pound Ridge stream that was hidden by thick woods at the edge of a long, yellowing meadow. I expressed concern that we might get lost, and J.C. had a ready solution: we could, he said, light small fires along the way and then stamp them out, leaving a trail of burn marks to guide our exit. What he didn't consider was how dry the meadow grass was and when he flicked his lighter and put the flame to dry tinder, the meadow exploded. The rapidly building fire was too dangerous to stamp out with our feet, so J.C. took out his fishing net and swatted at the fire. The netting erupted into flames and he was left holding a useless, circular metal hoop.

"Run!" he yelled, throwing the lighter as far as he could in an attempt hide the evidence.

We ran down the nearby country road, all the while yelling, "Fire! Fire! Fire!" We also concocted a story, which we later shared with responding fire crews. The story went like this: We were walking along the road and spotted the fire. We tried to put it out, we told them, and J.C. held up what was left of the fishing net as proof.

I don't know if the fire crews ever believed us, and I hope the statute of limitations has run out for such a crime; the fire consumed a fair number of acres. Fortunately for us, the entire area had already been designated for flooding to create a large reservoir. The burned land was going to be under water anyway.

The fire story is emblematic of my many stymied attempts to forge pathways in my life. In most cases, I have only myself to blame, and I could develop, as my adoptive mother did, a top ten list of perceived deficits:

1. *The fact that I am not particularly smart; I have merely worked hard to overcome my intellectual shortcomings.*
2. *The fact that I wasn't consistently a good husband—that I wasn't as loving and supportive as I should have been. I'll need to try harder if I get married again.*
3. *The fact that I had more than one marriage. Many, many more than one. There's no escaping the truth that there is personal failure attached to that record.*
4. *The fact that I am estranged from three of my children. The divorces didn't help and neither did my maniacal devotion to work. There's more to life than work-related achievements. I'm still hoping I can repair the relationships with my three sons. I do miss them.*
5. *The fact that I spent too many years trying to hide, instead of re-*

solve, my insecurities.

6. *The fact I am not very good about keeping in touch with friends. I seem to slide through life, one acquaintance or experience after another, and close doors when others open.*
7. *The fact that I seem sometimes to be off-putting to people when I am steadfastly arguing a point; I still don't know if this is my issue or theirs. It's probably more mine. I have, until very recently, equated being right with having worth. I'm getting better at letting things go.*
8. *The fact that I haven't made the best lifestyle choices, especially when it comes to diet. I'm tackling it still, bit by bit.*
9. *The fact that I ask too many questions, or so some people tell me. It is what I'm trained to do professionally, but in my personal life it sometimes stems from my need to know everything about a person so I can protect myself from harm.*
10. *The fact that this little exercise hurts because I realize there's more work to be done with me.*

The fire episode was also a harbinger of the chaos that was to envelope my life, fueled by a search for identity that always seemed to place me on the precipice of danger.

I had always been something of a white-knuckled airplane passenger, largely because I had no control over the flight. I also had a fear of falling from great heights. And so, I briefly took up skydiving near Loveland, Colorado, in the mid-1980s, making several tandem jumps from an airplane at the edge of the Front Range of the Rocky Mountains, the last one from two miles up. What better way to confront the fear of flying and falling, I thought, than to jump into nothingness on a wing and prayer, free-fall for a mile at more than 115 miles per hour, hope the chute opens after completing the look, reach, and pull protocol, and then glide to the ground.

My first dive was a Saturday jump from about ten thousand feet. My instructor, who had represented the U.S. in international competitions and had packed his red, white, and blue chute for our jump, hooked himself to my back. He was along for the ride to make sure I didn't panic or forget to pull the ripcord or, I suppose, pass out.

As we neared the point where hitting the drop zone was possible, I sat, legs dangling, in a large opening in the side of an old, noisy airplane. In that moment, I came to terms with my life and accepted the fact that one little miscue could be the end of it all. It was an interesting transformation in which I went from abject fear to adrenaline-fueled anticipation. I didn't want to die—in fact, I felt very much alive sitting there—but I was ready for death if that was in the cards.

My instructor counted backwards from ten. When he hit one, I leaned forward, fell, and caught a glimpse of the plane's tail as I zipped downward. I had been told by other veteran divers to make sure I looked at the majestic Front Range to the west, but I was more intent on trying to calm our buffeting by assuming a frog-like aerodynamic pose, then watching the altimeter strapped to my chest to make sure I pulled the ripcord at 5,200 feet. Never before or since have I been so focused on following instructions.

To my surprise, I didn't feel like I was falling, even though I was plummeting at roughly 200 feet per second toward terminal velocity. There was no stomach-in-the-throat sensation one gets from riding a roller coaster. Really, there was no discomfort at all. The brain, I later learned, has no nearby reference points in the sky from which to gauge altitude or speed.

At precisely 5,200 feet, I grabbed the handle of the ripcord and pulled, relieved to hear the parachute unfurl. A second or two later, a powerful force yanked us upward and then there was silence, save for the occasional light flapping of the chute. We were floating, high above and far removed from the bustle of everyday life. Below us, matchbox-sized cars moved in slow motion, their occupants going to work, running grocery errands or carting children to sporting events. I imagined the people in the doll house-sized buildings below us myopically focused on other ordinary tasks—paying bills, washing dishes, or doing laundry. And above it all, we soared, gloriously peaceful and unencumbered. The moment we landed, I wanted to go back up, and ever since that first dive I have looked at the sky differently. On good days, it is a friendly, wonderful place of solitude. And lo and behold, I no longer fear flying or falling.

For a short time in Colorado, I also spent Friday and Saturday evenings riding with a friend who was a county sheriff's officer. With the blessings of his supervisors, he unofficially deputized me, making me more than just a passenger. During one patrol, we chased a car thief who, in pitch-black darkness, bailed into a massive overgrown field at the end of a dead-end street. Another night, we responded to a large, rowdy party where a man had been stabbed in the arm; predictably, none of the drunken partygoers saw anything—or so they said. On yet another night, we calmed a nasty domestic dispute between a man and woman. She was leaving him and he was none too happy.

I think my friend got the better end of the deal with the domestic dispute. He shepherded the woman and her father as they shuttled back and forth through the front door, delivering her belongings to a car outside. I kept an eye on the husband, who sniped at them from the living room where he paced, agitated.

"You know your daughter was a stripper," he shouted at the father. "She's nothing but a slut."

"C'mon," I said, summoning an innate strength and looking at him squarely. "Don't do that. Nothing's gonna get solved right now."

He nodded. "Right. Yeah."

Moments later, he was at it again.

"You better not be taking any of my stuff you fuckin' whore."

"Seriously," I said, "that's enough. Sit down and let it go."

He looked at me angrily, weighing his options: Rush me or comply.

"Sit your ass down!" I said, pointing to a chair. "You can figure everything out later."

Thankfully, he sat down. I would not have relished a physical confrontation.

Later, I learned that at some point my friend's supervisor had pulled up outside to make sure everything was okay.

"How's your partner doing?" he had asked.

"Doing fine," my friend had said. "Everything's under control."

My friend's faith in me did wonders for my self-esteem. Not only did I learn to appreciate the difficult work of law enforcement, but I gained confidence that I can, in fact, bravely and decisively confront and survive things that may pose a significant threat to life and limb.

That included a short tenure teaching writing to male inmates at a county jail. The men were accused of or convicted of crimes ranging from theft to sexual assault to murder, and for one hour a week I sat in a room with them and encouraged them to be expressive in more constructive ways. I don't know how much they derived from the class; the diverse collection of inmates rarely completed weekly assignments, even though they had a lot of free time.

At one point, I remarked to one of the men—a heavily tattooed inmate accused of murder—that I would relish having as much time to write as he did. The inmate put a muscular arm around my shoulders, smiled and said, "We can arrange that for you if you want." Everyone laughed and the sense of brotherhood in that moment was alarming. I realized they could snuff me out in a heartbeat.

Most people, I suspect, don't need to resort to skydiving, playing cop, mingling with convicts, or hitchhiking across the country to build character and self-esteem. But I did. I needed to know what I was made of, what I was capable of, beneath the layers of insecurity.

My flirtations with chaos and danger were also part of my unsettled soul – one born of a dysfunctional childhood and the ever-present thought that, in the beginning, I was not wanted. As much as I'd always yearned to live, it occurs to me that the fight to survive was always closely followed by a death wish. That I believed it really wouldn't have mattered to anyone if I had died.

That realization came and then thankfully went when J.C. and I visited Pound Ridge together in the fall of 2019. We drove the hilly, winding roads. We pointed out the homes of the people we once knew or knew of. The diamonds where we played baseball. The schools where we labored to fit in. The forests we explored. Painful memories of parental abuse, peer ostracization, and a general sense of loneliness tugged at me initially. But gradually, I began to see the beauty of a place that had for decades been lodged in my memory as a dark, foreboding landscape left colorless by sheer unhappiness. For the first time, I had hope that—armed with the knowledge of my origins and beginning to form a more forgiving perspective of my life's journey—I could bury my dismal past. I could bury it right along with the damage done by the fire in the meadow, which sits somewhere below the large reservoir that swallowed it.

We drove past that reservoir too – and the ponds and lakes where we played ice hockey in the winters and fished in the summers. They looked lovely.

Chapter Eighteen

Lauren can't walk, she can't use her arms or hands, she can't talk, and her eyesight is significantly compromised. But she has the sweetest spirit, the prettiest smile, the heartiest laugh, the softest curly blonde hair, the most beautiful hazel eyes, and she can hear, extremely well. She instantly knows people by their voices and knows what they're saying, or at least understands the drift of it. And if you slip several fingers inside one of her curled hands—and she likes you—she'll squeeze as hard as she can.

Lauren has severe cerebral palsy, the result of being born at twenty-eight weeks weighing two pounds seven ounces, and suffering an extensive brain hemorrhage shortly after entering this life one Fourth of July. She is thirty years old now. For twenty-seven of those years, her mom, Lynn Shire, and Lynn's now ex-husband, John, cared for her in their homes. Today, their only child lives in a group home to help her adjust to life without her parents; they will not, after all, live forever.

Lauren visits frequently with her mom, her dad, and other relatives. She visits with me, too. That's because several months after Mary's death, I met Lauren and her mother and they welcomed me into their world, one that is loving, kind and uncommonly transparent.

To be embraced by such compassionate people was beyond my expectations, but the timing fit. It represented the culmination of my long journey toward self-identity.

Beyond offering me the purest kind of love, Lauren cemented my belief that people with physical or developmental disabilities are, almost without exception, more perfect than any of us can ever hope to be. They teach us humility, how to embrace joy in the little things, and how to live in the moment.

Lynn's unconditional love and acceptance of my rocky and rutted history, meanwhile, is not only heartwarming, it is helping me discover who I really am at my core and teaching me to love without fear, fail without retribution, and peel back and examine the layers of a life interrupted far too many times. I am no longer driven to chase a lofty image to present to the world. Lynn has lifted me into a new—and welcome—emotional universe.

Lynn's love and acceptance also carries a trust in me to help care for Lauren, whether it's supporting Lauren emotionally, carrying her from room to room, assisting with her tube feedings, or just being supportive of Lynn when Lauren is periodically hospitalized with pneumonia. Each time Lauren is hospitalized, Lynn worries that she will not survive.

It was, in fact, during one of Lauren's hospitalizations that Lynn and I had our first date. I had done something I'd never done before—subscribe to an online dating service. I wasn't looking for a serious relationship, just a friendship in the wake of Mary's death, and I was thoroughly enamored when I saw a picture of Lynn and Lauren smiling at each other. They were, I thought, two people I needed to get to know.

Lynn and I wrote each other through the dating site, talked a few times over the phone, then made plans to go to dinner on a Saturday night. But when that day arrived, Lynn called to say Lauren was in the hospital.

"You go ahead and keep the dinner reservation and take someone else," Lynn said.

"I'm not going to do that," I said. "I made the dinner reservation for us, not just anybody."

"Well, I suppose you could come to the hospital," she said, "although I haven't showered in two days and I'm not looking my best."

"If it will make you feel any better," I said, "I'll roll around in mud before I come up there."

She laughed, I went to the hospital, and we had dinner in the hospital cafeteria. It was a perfect first date, a perfect way to be introduced to two people who are inseparable and who have faced adversity with strength and courage.

I've always admired and felt protective of people with physical or developmental disabilities, and have railed at the cruel judgments they sometimes are forced to endure. My longtime friend, J.C., had a hip disorder (Perthes disease) in elementary school that required he wear a cumbersome leg brace and elevated shoe. I felt his frustration, understood his embarrassment, and marveled at his stubborn determination to plough through his disability.

A more gentle, gradual waltz of the sublime with the physically and developmentally challenged began when I was one of ten community members paired with Easterseals clients for a dancing-with-the-stars event. For several months, we practiced at a dance academy, and for those of us possessing marginal talents, it was a rigorous, frustrating experience. I do indeed dance like I have two left feet. What was most memorable, though, was watching the clients happily immerse themselves in the present. Most of them were genuinely joyful, unassuming, and determined to succeed at mastering dance. Not a single moment was taken for granted, and what nature had taken from some of them—the ability to analyze the details of one's life, project into the future, or languish in the past—was a gift. They rejoiced in being alive without nagging internal or external distractions. For an hour a week, they allowed us to also experience that freedom.

I have felt freedom from distractions at least four other times in my life, though I was often alone. In isolated Beaver Island, Michigan, I once took a walk along a bladder-rattling dirt road imprinted with the remains of long-departed frogs and snakes. The wind had disappeared in the twilight and the surrounding forest stood in almost complete silence, the only sound the crunch of my footsteps on the road's loose gravel. Years earlier, I had a similar experience when I pulled off a desolate road south of Rock Springs, Wyoming, exited the car, and felt the blistering heat of the day rising from the sandy soil. I heard nothing, not even from two horned antelope that stood like sentinels atop a small butte. I also found an oasis of calm on a ramshackle farm spread I once owned in Illinois. On evenings when the coyotes weren't yelping in the distance, I stood in the lighted space between the old smokehouse, chicken coop, listing barn, and crumbling concrete silo, imagining there was nothing outside of my little rural bubble. I had a similar experience on a visit to J.C.'s remote 120-acre spread in the wooded hills of east-central Vermont, where the silence was broken only by the occasional call of a crow or the bark of one of his Brittany Spaniels.

No clutter of humanity existed in these moments; no intruding technology or urgency to get everything done at once. Just time and nature, the recognition that life was once lived many years ago in the simplest of ways, and the fleeting hope that with practice, perhaps I could train myself to live happily, if only briefly, in the here and now.

Lauren seems to live that way—singularly focused on what is before her. When she hears my voice, she smiles, even if we're in different rooms. When someone misspeaks or makes a mistake, she laughs. When a person pays her a compliment, she doesn't just smile, she beams. Most of the time, she is happy.

Like the rest of us, she has moments of sadness. She frowns and sometimes cries when it comes time to say goodbye. Occasionally, the creases in her forehead tell you she is physically uncomfortable, or she doesn't like something you've said to her, or she's disturbed by testy interactions between people.

The one defining thing about Lauren, though, is that she is always present, always paying attention. It is a remarkable quality in a high-tech world that bombards us with myriad diversions every day.

Lauren and Lynn's sincere goodness and gentle spirit keep me grounded in the aftermath of my search, which answered so many questions, yet left so many more. One question that remains for all of us Shinns and Slocums is: What do we do with this new information moving forward?

I have solid relationships with my first cousin, Carol, and half-sister, Diane, that have grown into true friendships beyond our biological connection. I'm developing a promising relationship with my half-sister, Barbara, on my father's side. With my half-brothers—Eddie on my mother's side and Tommy on my father's— our connection may yet reach a full bloom. Barbara May's sister, Nancy, and I are polite and considerate to each other. I would like to get to know her better, although time may be running out for that; she is ninety now, barely survived complications from heart valve surgery, and is still fighting lung cancer. As for the rest of my biological family members, I don't yet know if relationships will develop. They are the ones who have chosen not to communicate with me or have stopped doing so.

Maybe it's too painful or confusing for some of my relatives to change their family's long-held narrative; maybe they remain unconvinced by the genetic evidence; maybe they don't like what they've heard about me from other family members. Or maybe they just don't care. I can't deny that this is painful, but I understand they have the right to live their lives however they choose, as if I'd never found them, if that's what they wish to do. There's no formula for how to adapt to the sudden appearance of a biological relative who, according to family history, isn't supposed to exist.

It's also possible they simply don't know how to move forward. I struggle with that too. We find ourselves in a situation where strangers are being introduced to each other and, even though they share DNA, they might as well not be related at all. They have no shared experiences, memories, histories, or loyalties to family ties. It's like being introduced to someone new at a social gathering, or workplace, or sporting event; we like that person or we don't or we're ambivalent. We find commonalities with that person or we discover none. We decide whether we want that person in our inner circle or remain a casual acquaintance. We also learn to accept it when a person distances themselves from us—something I'm learning to accept with some of my biological relatives.

Whatever rejection I have felt from those who have elected to stay on the sidelines is, thankfully, mostly a mild ache rather than a sting at this advanced stage of my life. It hurts, but it's not remotely close to crippling. Such rejection would have been far more difficult had I been rebuffed in my twenties or thirties, when the slightest hint of disapproval would have sent me circling the drain of self-doubt. Today, I can better appreciate someone's need to build personal boundaries, and I can celebrate when someone welcomes me into their world.

I came to these cathartic landing zones incrementally and I've been angry a few times, including once when I stood in my kitchen railing about those biological relatives who, by their actions or words, seemed to dismiss my existence or feelings. Beyond those who ignored me, some relatives also didn't want their last names in the book, some didn't want any mention of a mother or father, and one was angry at me that I knew more about Barbara May than they did.

This accumulation of rejections forced me to fully confront feelings of abandonment and reminded me that some people may still consider children born out of wedlock embarrassing products of a sin. I don't know if any of my biological relatives feel this way, but words like "illegitimate," "bastard," "stain," and "inferior" came to mind, and I wanted to scream all sorts of things at those who rebuffed me. "I didn't do this! I had no part in the creation of me!" I wanted to say. Or, "It's my story, too! It's my family, too!"

I nearly did scream at one biological relative in a text message, saying I felt like a stain. I added, "When will people walk outside of their own discomfort with the situation and think about what it must be like for me?" But the moment I sent it, I felt small and petty; fortunately, the relative responded compassionately: "You are not a stain. You are a human being, a child who was conceived by a woman and man who got together for reasons we don't know. Happens all the time... I have accepted you for a while now."

In the end, I agreed to change or exclude some relatives' names in the book to protect those who didn't want to be identified or shield those who I suspected would want to remain anonymous. But Barbara May's full name, her husband's name, the names of my biological father and adoptive parents, the name I was given at birth, and few other names—they are real. So too is the story. No one can take the story away from me. It belongs to me just as much as it does anyone else and it has comforted me.

Finding Barbara May and others in my biological family, finding Lynn and Lauren, has brought healing. In the 299 days it took to definitively discover Barbara May and my biological father, I became as close to whole as I've ever been. I reconciled with my past and embraced truths that only recently settled in my marrow.

Although much more conflicted, I was a bit like Barbara May in that I was a boy, and then a man, who was looking for love. What I didn't realize is that I was loved many times over by many people. I simply couldn't see it or couldn't believe it because I was blinded by my own feelings of inadequacy. That is one truth I've learned.

I can also now accept that I was a serviceable, hardworking journalist and author who didn't set the world on fire. I didn't win a Pulitzer. I didn't make it to the *New York Times* or the *Washington Post*. But the success I did achieve was a job well done. A book I wrote, *Crossing Over: One Woman's Escape from Amish Life*, was published by Harper Collins and was on the best-seller list in one Christian ranking; I had an essay published in *Home Again: Essays and Memoirs from Indiana* that also featured Kurt Vonnegut; and my brief musings about writing were featured in a Writer's Digest book called *Finding Your Voice*.

I also devoted considerable time to serving the communities where I lived, including the work with Easterseals; creating an organization in Illinois to support the educational futures of children from dysfunctional childhoods; volunteering with organizations combatting cancer and kidney disease, and teaching writing and oratory to young Fort Wayne students participating in an internationally known performing arts organization.

My adoptive mother never lived long enough to see most of those accomplishments, but I know she would have been proud. I think Barbara May would have been proud too.

I believe my adoptive mother also would have approved of my search for my birth mother. She gave me my adoption information knowing full well that I might use it to find my biological mother one day. She was confident, I think, that even if I found my birth mother, I would continue to love and appreciate her. And I do. I now know, too, that Barbara May would have welcomed me had I found her before she died.

I am extraordinarily lucky to have been loved by two mothers—one up close and one from afar. I also had two fathers, one of whom sounds like he was a good deal nicer than the one I lived with for the first seventeen years of my life. I'd like to think James Sr. would have embraced me.

One thing I've been doing a lot of lately is thinking about a woman's right to choose the fate of her unborn child. I have always supported that right generally, skirting the contentious debate about the timing of an abortion. But more than ever it is my hope that most women will choose adoption, as Barbara May did, if they believe they will be unable to care for the child. It is also my hope that our nation will continue to provide the kinds of pre-natal services that will help a woman care for herself and for the unborn child in her womb and post-natal services that will help the woman raise the child and have access to birth control. Some of us adoptees do turn out okay.

My belief in a woman's right to choose was tested three times in my life. One wife (we were on the verge of divorce) and two girlfriends had abortions—and one of the girlfriend's abortions was self-induced. The girlfriend never elaborated on how she induced a miscarriage, other than to say she "stuck something up there."

With all three abortions, I was the father, was willing to share the responsibility for the child, and had hoped abortion would not be the choice. With all three, I was reminded that, but for my birth mother's choice, I would not be around.

In my more fanciful, idle moments removed from such weighty topics, I delight in the notion that while I believe I can still be counted as a New Yawker, I am also a Jersey Boy. For me, that conjures up images not of Bruce Springsteen but of Frankie Valli and those nostalgic Four Seasons melodies. I am intrigued, too, by New Jersey folklore dating to the 1700s that I stumbled across along the way: Molly Pitcher, who purportedly carried pitchers of water to soldiers during the Revolutionary War's Battle of Monmouth, and the Jersey Devil, a hideous-looking flying creature with hooves and bat-like wings.

I am equally fascinated by the racing history of my birth mother's side of the family. Even though I spent my life wholly disinterested in car racing, when someone complains about my driving, I tell them proudly, "You do know, don't you, that I come from a family of race car drivers?" The response is usually a dramatic roll of the eyes.

As the pieces of my genetic puzzle began coming together, I was also struck by the interconnectedness of humanity. My ancestry.com profile, which initially showed 270 fourth cousins or closer, was at 800 and counting two years later, and included people from lands far from America's shores. And that's just those who had submitted their DNA to the database and not counting scores of distant relatives. Among the latter was a distant cousin from Scotland, Elaine, who emailed me to say she had added my name to her family tree.

The truth is that there are parts of each of us all over the world in the DNA of scores of people and, scientists have determined, emanating from a racially diverse melting pot of ancient bloodlines. That means that when we focus on our differences, we are, at least genetically, often at odds with ourselves. We are ignoring the idea that we are, loosely interpreting, all brothers and sisters, linked intricately by molecules and cells and chromosomes. We are much more alike than we are different. And we are, I suspect, prone to forgetting that we are all looking for the same things at one point or another, including a sense of home.

I am so grateful I have lived long enough to find my home, a place of belonging that is more than a building or a street address or a point on a map. I believe the essence of home is finding ourselves and loving what we've found. It is the knowledge that those closest to us not only love us but have our backs.

I've learned to see the totality of my life and be comfortable with all of it, even the rough patches. I can say with conviction, "I've had a good run." Or as my adoptive mother wrote late in life in the poem *When Comes My Day*: "Our blessings far outnumbered woes."

I can bask in the love of Lynn and Lauren and Amber and Carol and Diane and J.C. and the many others who have befriended me and loved me, even when I didn't love myself. Some of them have held me in their hearts for decades, including one woman who promised my adoptive mother a quarter of a century ago she would always look out for me. That person has never wavered.

I can also now bask in the love of Barbara May. We were, after all, one once, joined in the most intimate of ways for nine months.

I hope that my birth mother found love in the way I finally have. Undisturbed. Tranquil. Forgiving. I hope that she died knowing that she was not only loved by many, but especially by one blue-eyed baby boy named Richard Alan Shinn and by the man he became.

My first cousin, Carol, and half-sister, Diane, think Barbara May and I will meet again one day in the afterlife. I don't know if that's possible, but it is a warm, pleasant thought. It would be great to see my birth mother again.

In the meantime, I will make do with the five pictures of Barbara May as a young child, a teenager and a young adult, thoughtfully arranged in a wooden frame (a gift from Carol), and a picture of Barbara May shortly before she died (a gift from Diane).

They are pictures of a life I never knew, and some of them were taken on the cusp of a birth I cannot recollect. But I cherish those pictures, I cherish Barbara May, and every so often I look at them, drift into a consciousness removed from distraction, and speak silently to her.

Thank you, Mom. Thank you for loving me. Thank you for giving me life.

Chapter Nineteen

December 2019

Dear Mom,

It feels really good to say that. Mom. And to say it with conviction. I never knew how meaningful it would be to find you until the opportunity presented itself. I am so very, very fortunate and grateful—even if there are some things about you I may never know.

My only regret is that, now that I know who you are, I can't invite you over for coffee, or call you on the phone to chatter about the mundane, or take a road trip, just the two of us, to an interesting locale.

And I would have loved to have had you at the wedding of Lynn and I, which was a simple ceremony in Lynn's lavishly planted backyard conducted by one of Lynn's sisters. Some say seven is a lucky number. For me, I believe it is.

Later, Lynn and I flew to Florida, where we settled in on Captiva Island for a few sweltering days of exploring the Gulf of Mexico and mangroves-lined Pine Island Sound for manatees, dolphins, seabirds, and seashells—and sampling far too much of the local cuisine while pushing aside the heat with frozen piña coladas.

Many of the shells we collected—conches, olives, scallops, and cockles—were near perfect, but some Lynn had gathered and kept were broken.

At one point, I asked her, "Why are you keeping the broken ones?"

"Just because they're broken doesn't mean they're not beautiful," she chirped, sunny smile and all.

Her response could have been a pleasant metaphor for all sorts of things. For me for most of my life. For you, I imagine, and for my adoptive mother. For Lauren. For anyone and anything that carries the scars of life.

The beauty of brokenness is somewhat of a revelation for me.

Another good thing that has happened along the way to finding you is that I am getting better at following late author Richard Carlson's admonition: "Don't Sweat the Small Stuff... and it's all small stuff." I'm not sure about the last part. It seems a bit too sweeping. But a good deal of what we agonize about in life is, in fact, relatively insignificant. Moreover, much of what confronts us we have no control over. That includes the decision by some of my newfound relatives to discount my existence.

Carol recently sent me a picture of your other four children, who had gathered for a wedding in New Jersey. They were all smiling—Diane, Lisa, Jeanne, and Eddie—and they were all dressed in their finest. My first thought was, "It would have been nice to be in that picture with them." My second thought was, "At least two of them don't know what they're missing. I'm a good person to know." That's progress for me in valuing self.

Moreover, even if some of them never come around to acknowledging my existence, they will never be able to take you away from me. Nor can they stop me from claiming their family tree as mine too. That was brought into high relief when I filled out the marriage license application for Lynn and me. The county clerk's office asked for information about our parents for genealogy purposes and office officials said I could choose either my adoptive or biological parents. I chose you and my biological father. For the first time in my life on a legal document, I put down Barbara May Shinn and James Russell Slocum. I did it because my true genealogy lies with the two of you. I also did it because it allowed me to claim the two of you as a part of me. And that, I guess, officially brought us full circle, the three of us. Back to the beginning. Back to my beginning.

I am not forsaking my adoptive parents. They raised me, and my adoptive mother loved me. But I will also have a place for my biological parents, especially you.

Shortly before my adoptive mother died, she told me that if I ever needed her, she would be sitting on my shoulder, available for comfort or consultation. It's a good thing I have two shoulders, Mom, because I have reserved a space for you on the other one.

All my love,
Your son

Epilogue

I hardly knew long-distance running star Dave Pottetti and I hadn't thought much about him since he killed himself half a century ago at the age of twenty-two. But for reasons I couldn't understand initially, images of him running with graceful strides along the narrow winding roads of my hometown in Westchester County flooded back to me as I ran headlong into my search for my biological mother. I remembered, too, the few times he encouraged me to run with him.

As the memories of Dave surfaced, so too did this question: Was he running toward or away from something? It is a question I've often asked of myself in a more figurative sense and in both of our cases it turns out it may have been a bit of both.

I discovered the parallels between his early life and mine were similar, although I didn't share his running prowess, his academic achievement, or his tragic end. We both came from abusive, dysfunctional families headed by intellectual parents who didn't know how to raise children. We both felt isolated from the rest of the world. We experienced depression, distrust of others, and difficulty socializing. We searched for self in a society turned upside down by cultural upheaval and found escape in drugs. And through it all, we shared an affinity for the woods, for animals, for all things nature.

His sister, Sara Wright, almost four years older than the brother she called Davey, told me the story of his short life. Sara, now in her seventies, struggled with the same challenges as her brother, and she ultimately turned to a lifelong romance with nature as a balm against the wounds she and Davey suffered as children. She is a naturalist with a doctorate in ethology—the study of wild animals in their natural environment. She has also become an advocate for the empowerment of women and has worked as crisis counselor.

From the beginning, Sara considered herself Davey's protector. She recalls climbing into his crib and wrapping her arms around him. Later, she tried to shield him in other ways from the household chaos.

Their father, she said, was an Italian immigrant, an aeronautical engineer, and an emotionally arrested rage-a-holic who nevertheless loved his children deeply. Their artist mother grew up in privilege, and was cold, distant, and punitive when the children disagreed with her. The parents drank heavily. They argued often. They emotionally abused Davey and Sara.

"We grew up in a crazy household," Sara said, "that looked good on the outside and was insane on the inside."

She and Davey alternately spent time in their parents' Pound Ridge home and the nearby home of their maternal grandmother and her husband. The siblings felt safest at their grandparents' house and they felt safest together. They were best friends and inseparable growing up, and at the same time isolated from the rest of the world.

"Neither one of us," Sara said, "was able to form a really close bond with other people. You don't grow up in a situation like we did and trust people. So we created our own little world and nature was such an important part of it."

Sara and Davey spent much of their childhood in the woods around their parents' home, their grandparents' pre-revolutionary house and 50-acre spread, and the nearby Ward Pound Ridge Reservation, a roughly 4,000-acre county park. They climbed and swung on large, twisting vines dangling from trees. They went exploring for all manner of wild animals: skunks and squirrels and raccoons and birds. They camped out sometimes. The woods were sanctuaries, places away from family dysfunction.

Sara and Davey also ran together. It was an activity Davey loved. But after his death, Sara realized Davey may have also been running away from the problems at home and towards a kinder existence. "He was," she eventually concluded, "running for his life."

Running was never about achieving fame, although the more Davey ran, the more the medals and trophies piled up. As a distance running star at Fox Lane

High School, Davey won the National Schoolboy Championship and set the state high school record in the two-mile run. A time he set as a Fox Lane harrier at the famed Van Cortlandt Park in Bronx, New York, in 1966 still stands as one of the top one hundred cross country marks for that course.

No fewer than forty-two colleges and universities offered Davey scholarships before he graduated Fox Lane. He ultimately chose Harvard and became a star there too. In 1968, he and Yale's Frank Shorter, a future Olympic gold medalist, were named Cross Country All-Americans. Davey also set a school record in the steeplechase at the Penn Relays that stood for twenty-six years.

He had his sights set on the 1972 Olympics when suddenly, after his sophomore year, he quit the Harvard team. He told his coach and others that he no longer found joy in running, that he had stuck with it in the final years only to please his family, and that he was now interested in exploring spiritual matters and learning how to be more social. Regarding running, he said, "I can't try for something I don't want anymore."

Sara and Davey shared a bit of Native American ancestry, and Davey spent several summers during college visiting Navajo reservations in Arizona and Yaqui tribes in Mexico. There he explored Native American culture and re-discovered his love of nature. He also experimented with two nature-born psychedelic drugs: peyote and psilocybin. Native Americans have long used such drugs for ceremonial and curative purposes and to try to achieve a stronger interconnectedness with the universe. Davey, Sara speculated, discovered an alternate mystic world in the drugs' hallucinations and euphoria that he much preferred to the real world, where he had labored for so many years under the weight of stardom and the pressure to succeed at virtually everything.

The trouble was, when he came down from his psychedelic experiences, he had no stable platform on which to land. No family harmony. Isolation from others. An unfinished understanding of the arc of his life and the larger framework of its ebb and flow. It also didn't help that he was a very sensitive, introverted person. Real life was sometimes painful for him.

He graduated from Harvard in 1971 with a bachelor's in sociology and then returned to his parents' house in Pound Ridge. There he built a Navajo Hogan—a traditional dwelling—out of deerskin, complete with a stone fire pit. He alternately lived in the Hogan and a room in his parents' house. He took a part-time job with a local contractor.

In November 1971, he traveled to Southport Island, Maine to visit Sara—a trip he made often. Sara was then a waitress and divorced mother of two. Sara remembers she and Davey sitting by the fireplace and Davey at one point saying, "I'm so tired. I'm just so tired. I've done everything I wanted to do. I've been everywhere. I've seen everything." Earlier, he had also told her that the only reason Harvard had wanted him was for his running, not for who he was as a person.

In one of the greatest regrets of her life, Sara lit into her younger brother that night by the fireplace. "How can you think like this?" she said. "You have your whole life ahead of you." She was reacting out of fear, but in the ensuing years she realized that, in that moment, when her brother most needed compassionate guidance, she had behaved like her judgmental, punitive mother.

The following month, Sara saw Davey again during a Christmas visit to Pound Ridge. He seemed more peaceful. He had grown his hair long, wore long flowing clothes, and didn't appear to be stoned. During that visit, brother and sister went to the nearby reservation, just like they had when they were children. As they walked the woods, Davey, referring to Sara by her nickname, said, "Oh Bibi, we had the most wonderful childhood, didn't we?" He sounded wistful and was clearly ignoring the turmoil of their younger years. It was as if he felt they would never be able to recapture the good times they shared when they were able to escape the family squalls.

After that Christmas visit, in January 1972, Davey called Sara in Maine one evening and wanted to talk about a skunk he had befriended and let into his parents' house without their knowledge. The skunk was living in the closet of Davey's room and he was worried his parents would find out about it. He was hoping he could keep the animal a secret until the next day, when his parents would leave for a vacation. Nothing seemed out of the ordinary with Davey. Just typical Davey. Mingling with the animals.

Sara couldn't have imagined that twenty-four hours later, when Davey should have been going to his grandparents' house for dinner, he drank a cup of peyote tea, walked into the Hogan, and put a bullet in his head. He had purchased the gun in November—the same month he had told his sister he was tired of living.

In hindsight, Sara said, she should have seen how dire the warning signs were in Davey's words, but she didn't. It haunts her to this day.

After Davey's death, his family barely mentioned him. His father burned the Hogan in the driveway of the family home and took pictures of the remains. The pictures were stored in a box that contained a metal can holding Davey's ashes. The box was tucked away in the family attic for more than three decades.

Sara, meanwhile, has no idea what became of Davey's running medals, a detail she finds "unspeakably horrible." It was as if all things Davey had been wiped away. It was as if he had never existed.

Davey's death and the family silence plunged Sara into what she calls "The Dead Years"—a ten-year stretch during which she went through the motions of life without being truly present. She periodically medicated herself with alcohol and suffered from agoraphobia. Eventually, she was diagnosed with PTSD and acute anxiety disorder. She began focusing her attention on the one thing that had brought her and Davey comfort—nature.

In her later years, she has split her time between a 600-square-foot log cabin on 20 acres in western Maine and an adobe dwelling in Abiquiu in northern New Mexico with a view of the Sangre de Cristo Mountains.

Sara writes passionately in professional journals, international women's publications, and a blog about myriad subjects, including sunrises and sunsets, the relationships between humans and nature, the interconnectedness of animals and plants through time and space, the rape of the land and of women, and occasionally about her journey from the depths of despair. With her writing, she often includes photographs of what she observes in the natural world. She is ever-thinking, ever-experiencing, ever-reaching for life's meaning.

Sara received a measure of closure in 2003 when Davey's ashes were found in the Pound Ridge attic and given to her. She buried them beside a brook on her Maine property. A Red-tailed Hawk, Davey's favorite bird of prey, appeared on a nearby branch during the private ceremony. Sara believes it was Davey paying a visit. Such is her belief in mystical forces that guide our lives.

It could be, I now realize, that those same forces may have revived my memories of Dave during the search for my birth mother—to serve as a stark reminder that we are, all of us, engaged in a search for self and meaning beyond the superficial. That even those people we revere struggle to achieve equilibrium.

When Dave encouraged me to run with him on the back roads of Pound Ridge, it's possible that he sensed I was like him in many ways; that his was an act of one lost soul trying to lift the lost soul of another. That, Sara said, would be in keeping with the part of Dave few people knew. Though he was not yet fully formed, he was, she said, compassionate, kind, and possessing uncommon decency. He was more than a string of statistics.

I am also struck by the possibility that had I not chosen to immerse myself in this world and fight tooth and nail to learn how to live with humans, I might have withdrawn, much the way Dave did. I might even have chosen to check out. I'd like to believe that if Dave had persevered, he would have found himself, as I finally have.

I may never again isolate myself in nature like I did in my troubled youth, as Dave did. I have become, for better or worse, a creature of the human world. But I have also been reminded in my recounting of my life that in nature there is always the promise of a better tomorrow. And for the first time in a long, long time, I can hear—really hear—the crows, jays, chickadees, nuthatches, sparrows, cardinals, and bluebirds. I can marvel at a brilliant morning sun bursting through a labyrinth of tree branches, or a pastel sky of pinks and purples in repose at dusk. I can smell the earth in fallen leaves and mossy growths after an evening rain. I can see all of life, then and now, with clarity.

The now is not always rosy. My joints hurt when I wake in the morning. My left knee, repaired with arthroscopic surgery more than twenty years ago, is starting to feel rubbery again. The right one is acting up too. And my energy levels seem to wane some days. It is the inevitable wearing out process, I suppose.

But I choose to keep going and it has been more than worth it. The inexorable reality, for me at least, is that after the storms of life pass and somewhere over the emerging rainbows, the clouds do indeed fall behind us and bluebirds do fly.

Acknowledgments

I am indebted to the people who walked all or parts of this journey with me. Their guidance, research, or words of encouragement were invaluable.

Besides those already mentioned, I am especially grateful for the passionate, insightful prodding of my primary editor, Amy Grier, who encouraged me to explore circumstances I'd just as soon forget, and the ever-present sharp-witted suggestions of work colleague Rachel Blakeman.

Others contributing in ways large and small included Bonnie Penhollow, who came alongside me in a particularly dark hour; Neil Hill, who went out of his way to confirm a recollection; Dale Buuck, who took an early interest in my search and suggested genealogical possibilities; Carole Ann Moore, who has always been supportive of my writing; Gary and Pattie Gatman, who have my back no matter what; Tracie Martin, whose kindness touched me in the places that needed it; Glenda Ford, who has never given up on me even when she had every reason to; Eric Olson, a great storyteller whose curiosity about my journey goes beyond his journalistic undertakings; and Dr. Basil Genetos, my longtime cardiologist who not only has helped keep me alive but who has also expressed interest in my writing.